ARTHURIAN TRADITION
 a beginner's guide

CLAIRE HAMILTON

Hodder & Stoughton
A MEMBER OF THE HODDER HEADLINE GROUP

Acknowledgements

The author would like to thank all those who have provided copyright material used in this book.

I would particularly like to thank Jane Brideson of Dark Moon Designs for her illustrations. Also Sophie Woodrow for copying the crowns for Authur's Shield, on p. 51.

Every effort has been made to contact all the holders of copyright material but if any have been inadvertently overlooked, the publisher will be pleased to make the necessary amendments at the first available opportunity.

Orders: please contact Bookpoint Ltd, 39 Milton Park, Abingdon, Oxon OX14 4TD. Telephone: (44) 01235 827720, Fax: (44) 01235 400454. Lines are open from 9.00–6.00, Monday to Saturday, with a 24 hour message answering service. Email address: orders@bookpoint.co.uk

British Library Cataloguing in Publication Data
A catalogue record for this title is available from The British Library

ISBN 0 340 781467

First published 2000
Impression number 10 9 8 7 6 5 4 3 2 1
Year   2005 2004 2003 2002 2001 2000 1999

Copyright © 2000 Claire Hamilton

Typeset by Transet Limited, Coventry, England.
Printed in Great Britain for Hodder & Stoughton Educational, a division of Hodder Headline plc, 338 Euston Road, London NW1 3BH by Cox and Wyman Limited, Reading, Berks.

CONTENTS

Chapter 6   Courtly Love   55

Chapter 7   Love triangles   63

Chapter 8   The role of women   73

INTRODUCTION

Wise druids, prophesy to Arthur
what will be, what is,
what was once perceived.

These lines, spoken by the great bard Taliesin in the Dark Ages, echo down the centuries to us today. Taliesin was Arthur's contemporary and once travelled with the king and his warriors in a magic ship to the Kingdom of *Annwn*, the Celtic Underworld, to bring back the most precious object in the world. It was a pearl-rimmed cauldron guarded by nine priestesses. Only seven warriors returned, Taliesin among them, and what happened to the cauldron is not yet known.

This is one of the first and strangest stories of Arthur, and it is found in early Welsh poetry. Although it belongs in some part to history, in some to mythology, it contains ancient truths which still have meaning for us. But what these are can be understood only after making a proper assessment of Arthur. His image has, after all, gone

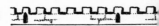

through many transformations over the centuries – Celtic warlord, figurehead of courtly chivalry, mystical archetype, and national hero.

To find the true meaning of Arthur, and of the great body of Arthurian legends known as the Matter of Britain, we must find out who Arthur was in history, who he is in legend, where he got his reputation, why he is such an attractive and compelling figure, and how he changes in each age. Only then can we begin to realize the great heritage he has given us and, more importantly, what he offers us today.

who was arthur?

This chapter looks at the historical sources, the material which had been most hotly debated by Arthurian scholars the world over. Some of them feel we have firm evidence of his existence, some grudgingly admit there may be some truth to him, and one or two consider him completely mythical. Let us examine the evidence for ourselves.

The lines at the beginning of the Introduction, taken from the thirteenth-century *Cad Goddau* (The Battle of the Trees), are among several early mentions of Arthur, all in Welsh poems. A further reference is found in the *Y Gododdin*, believed to have been spoken by another bard, Aneurin:

He charged before three hundred of the finest,
He cut down both centre and wing,
He excelled in the forefront of the noblest host,
He gave gifts of horses from the herd in winter.
He fed black ravens on the rampart of a fortress
Though he was no Arthur.
Among the powerful ones in battle,
In the front rank, Gwawrddur was a palisade.

This suggests that Arthur's name was well known and used as a yardstick for prowess from earliest times. It can be taken to show that the legendary Arthur of medieval chivalry was based on a solid historical figure – unless, as some scholars fear, it was a later interpolation in the manuscript.

Another intriguing reference is in the *Stanzas of the Graves* found in the medieval *Black Book of Carmarthen*:

There is a grave for March, a grave for Gwythur,
A grave for Gwgawn Red-sword;
Wonder unknown, a grave for Arthur.

This suggests that Arthur's grave cannot be found and helps to foster the enduring belief that Arthur never died but waits for the call to return again and defend this island in its hour of need.

It is important to remember that the Welsh literature which contains these references, although written down between the eleventh and fourteenth centuries by Christian monks, records oral histories that date from at least five hundred years earlier. During this period, the time of the so-called Dark Ages, stories had already grown up around the figure of Arthur – which is why it is so difficult to disentangle the historical Arthur from the legendary one.

Duke of Battles

All the evidence we have for the historical Arthur suggests he was a Celtic warrior living in either the fifth or sixth century CE. The earliest historical (as opposed to poetical) reference to him is in the *Historia Brittonum*, written by a monk called Nennius, at the beginning of the ninth century. Nennius says that huge numbers of Saxons were invading Britain and that Arthur fought them along with the British kings. He calls Arthur their *dux bellorum* (duke of battles). He then lists twelve battles of which the last and bloodiest was the battle of Mount Badon – in which Arthur killed 960 men, apparently singlehandedly!

There is also an entry in the tenth-century copy of monastic Easter tables, the *Annals of Wales*, stating that the battle of Badon took place in 516 and that in it Arthur carried the image of the Virgin Mary on his shoulders for three days and nights (for 'shoulders' read 'shield', and see Chapter 5), and that the Britons were the victors. A further entry tells of the battle of Camlann 'in which Arthur and

Medraut (Mordred) perished'. None of these references, however, is completely reliable and none of them calls Arthur a king.

ARTHUR AND GWLADYS

Arthur also features in some of the Welsh Saints' *Lives*. There is a revealing early tale in the eleventh-century *Life of St Cadoc* in which Cadoc tells how his future mother Gwladys (Gladys) elopes with the King of Glamorgan. Arthur is playing dice on a hilltop with his companions Cai and Bedwyr (later to become Sir Kay and Sir Bedivere) when Gwladys appears riding on a horse with the king. Arthur takes a fancy to her but is reminded by his friends of their duty to help those in distress:

> *Behold, three noble heroes, Arthur and his two companions Cai and Bedwyr, were sitting on a hilltop, playing dice. When they saw the king and the girl, Arthur's heart was filled with desire. Full of bad thoughts, he said to his companions: 'I am burning with desire for the maiden whom that warrior is carrying on his horse.' But they answered: 'You mustn't do anything so unlawful; we are supposed to help those in distress and need. Let us help these people who need succour.' Arthur replied 'Very well, if you would rather help him than secure the maiden for me, go and ask on whose land they are fighting.'*[1]

This story not only makes Arthur seem like a more human chieftain who has to grapple with his natural desires, but also illustrates the ideal of chivalry in its Celtic and, perhaps embryonic, form.

In another tale, the Breton *Life of St Illtud*, Illtud claims to be Arthur's cousin and says that as a young man he joined Arthur's army.

ARTHUR THE TYRANT

In some of the *Lives* Arthur is referred to as *Tyrannus*. This might not mean he was a tyrant; it could simply mean that he gained his

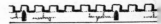

rulership by military prowess instead of constitutional right. It is noticeable that in these stories the saints are depicted as outwitting Arthur without actually overthrowing him. This could have been a clever publicity exercise. If Arthur was already a considerable figure in folklore then it would be prestigious for the saints to outwit him. Another possibility is that it could reflect tension between Arthur and the Church. Although he was considered to be on the same side as the Church, as a secular ruler he might at times have come into conflict with Church authority. This could explain why he is called *rex rebelliosus* (the rebellious king) in *The Life of St Gildas* written by Caradoc in 1130.

Gildas the Miserable

Gildas himself was a rather negative and quarrelsome character who wrote *De Excidio Britanniae* (*The Ruin of Britain*) around 540 CE in which he laments the havoc and ruin caused by the Saxons. In it he claims to have been born in the same year as the Battle of Badon, but curiously he makes no mention of Arthur. Gildas' silence is extremely problematical for Arthurian scholars. Needless to say, various explanations have been offered. One is that his work was purely ecclesiastical and therefore not concerned with the exploits of Arthur. Another is that Arthur killed one of Gildas' brothers because he refused to submit to his authority and kept raiding villages, whereupon Gildas reacted by throwing his account of Arthur into the sea.

The Battle of Badon Hill

From these historical accounts it is at least certain that the Battle of Badon Hill took place. It was the last of a series of battles against the Saxons and the decisive one. At least one account, as we have seen, credits the outcome entirely to Arthur. It consisted of a three-day siege by Arthur and a band of mounted cavalry. The slaughter

was appallingly heavy but at least it secured peace for the next forty years.

There is still much debate about the location of Badon Hill. Possibilities include a site near Swindon Gap, Little Solsbury Hill near Bath, and the iron-age fort known as Badbury Rings in Dorset. Nothing can be said for certain but at least there is agreement that it must have been in the South-West.

The siting of the Battle of Camlann, at which Arthur was killed, is equally uncertain. Suggested sites include Slaughter Bridge on the River Camel in Cornwall, Camelon near Falkirk in Scotland, and Camboglanna, a fort on Hadrian's Wall.

Tintagel

Situated on a rocky promontory on the north coast of Cornwall, the craggy and romantic castle at Tintagel is traditionally regarded as the place where Arthur was conceived. Because Geoffrey of Monmouth's account was considered fictional, it was thought unlikely that evidence would be found for this. However, archaeological research has shown that Tintagel was a Celtic fortified site and may also have been a Roman trading station.

Tintagel was possibly the most important site in Cornwall and could certainly have been used by an important chieftain in Arthur's time. In fact as recently as 1998 archaeologists unearthed a stone fragment there inscribed: 'Artognou father of a descendant of Coll had this made.' Needless to say, while its authenticity is not in doubt, whether it constitutes proof of the legendary Arthur is being debated.

Cadbury Castle

The huge hill-fort near South Cadbury, known as Cadbury Castle, was the location of Arthur's court of Camelot, according to the antiquarian John Leland, writing in 1542. It has four lines of bank-and-ditch

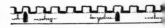

defence which were once surrounded by dense woodland. Leslie Alcock's recent excavations in the 1960s revealed the post holes of what would have been a great wooden hall, measuring 60 by 30 feet (18 by 9 metres), and standing on the high part of the hill where Arthur's Palace had traditionally been located. It would have been surrounded by a stone and timber defensive wall with a watchtower on it. Nearby are the remains of a Roman-style gatehouse. These findings show that the hilltop was refortified in 470 CE, a date which would certainly have been contemporary with Arthur.

GLASTONBURY

In 1190 a hollow tree-trunk was unearthed in the precincts of Glastonbury Abbey and found to contain the gigantic body of a man together with that of a woman who retained a plaited length of blonde hair. A monk grabbed the hair and, of course, it immediately disintegrated in his hands. Beneath the makeshift grave was a stone and underneath that a lead cross with the Latin inscription: *Hic jacet sepultus inclitus Rex Arturus, in insula Avalonia*, 'Here lies entombed the renowned King Arthur in the isle of Avalon'.

Gerald of Wales was the first to record this find. Seizing on the fact that William of Malmesbury had once called Glastonbury *Ynis Witrin* (the Glass Island), he became convinced that Glastonbury and Avalon were one and the same. But William of Malmesbury, who researched long and hard, could find no connection between Arthur and Glastonbury.

In fact, Gerald was probably being over-enthusiastic because the supposed finding of Arthur's grave was suspicious on several counts. Firstly, it was beneficial to the monarchy, who could happily embrace the myth of Arthur if he was no longer expected to return at any minute with a conquering army from Wales. Secondly the sudden fame and revenue it produced for the Abbey allowed for vital rebuilding as well as making it an important place of pilgrimage. Thirdly, the fact that Arthur was called a king in the inscription was odd considering he was known as duke or emperor in Celtic times.

All in all there were too many questions to be answered and the idea of Arthur's tomb was finally discredited. Nevertheless, the link between Arthur and Glastonbury remains to this day.

This is not entirely surprising, for Arthur already had a link with Glastonbury. In his *Life of Gildas* Caradoc tells how King Melvas, who reigned in the summer country, abducted Gwenhwyfar (Guinevere) and how, after searching for a year, Arthur finally located her at Glastonbury. He raised a huge army to besiege the island but, before battle could begin, the Abbot stepped in and negotiated her peaceful return. He also received compensation from both kings for violating the sacredness of the place.

Celtic Otherworldly islands

The story of Melvas has strong overtones of the Celtic Otherworld – a beautiful world, existing in parallel to this one, in which time seems to stand still. The abduction of Guinevere for a year by a king associated with summer suggests a ritual seasonal theme similar to that of Persephone's abduction by Hades. The sacredness of the island links it with Celtic Otherworld islands, such as *Tir n'an Og* (the Land of Youth), and Guinevere becomes a type of nature goddess reminiscent of Blodeuwedd, the flower bride, in the tale of Math from the *Mabinogion*.

In the *Matter of Britain*, as the legends of Arthur came to be called, the Celtic myth of the regenerated nature goddess goes hand in hand with the archetypal myth of the returning hero. It is the power of this ancient mythology that makes Arthur such an enduring figure, towering even over later heroes such as King Alfred the Great.

THE GROWTH OF
A LEGEND

A s we have seen, Arthur, as Celtic hero, had become a legendary
figure well before the French romances took hold of him. The
ideals of chivalry which grew up around him were also originally
Celtic, as was his identification with the land. Added to this, the use
of magical weapons, the idea of the elevated status of women, and
the undertaking of the spiritual quest, were also deep-rooted Celtic
concepts.

CELTIC BELIEFS

The Celts had a particular regard for the imagination. Their world
rested on the power of symbolism, which for them had links with
spirituality and with the realm of the Otherworld. Their tales were
multi-layered in meaning, reflecting their understanding that they
lived in two worlds at once, the sacred and the secular. This affected
how they behaved in battle. Their belief in the transmigration of the
soul after death made their warriors, both male and female,
uncommonly brave. Proud and fierce, they fought naked, unafraid of
death. In their eyes Arthur represented the perfect hero.

TALES FROM THE MABINOGION

Some of the earliest Celtic prose tales of Arthur are found in the
collection of Welsh myths made by Lady Charlotte Guest in the mid-

nineteenth century, which she called the *Mabinogion*. Probably the earliest in which Arthur features is *Culhwch and Olwen*, in which Arthur helps Culhwch to achieve a list of impossible tasks set by the giant Ysbaddaden for the winning of his daughter Olwen.

This tale is full of wit and riddling in true Celtic style. The list of Arthur's followers is exhaustive and comical, containing some characters who seem to be pure invention, such as Sgilti Light Foot who could run along reed-tops without bending them. Arthur helps Culhwch in the tasks laid on him, especially in hunting down the enchanted boar Twrch Trwyth for the three treasures between his ears – razor, comb and shears.

The fact that Ysbaddaden is fated to die when his daughter marries shows that this tale harks back to myths linked to primitive seasonal rituals. These typically have an older man challenged and killed by a younger rival in the contest for a young maiden. In other words, the maiden, Nature, must be rescued from the clutches of Winter so that the earth can be refertilized.

The Dream of Rhonabwy, in which Arthur also features, is even stranger than *Culhwch and Olwen*. In fact the whole story is one long dream riddled with symbolism for which, as the author admits at the end, a code is needed. The dreamer, Rhonabwy, is a medieval character, for this was written in the thirteenth century. Yet he receives his dream through the Celtic practice of sleeping on a bull's hide. (Druids commonly used this method to summon a prophetic message for the whole village.)

In the dream Rhonabwy is transported to the River Severn, where Arthur is playing a boardgame called *gwyddbwyll* with a chieftain named Owein, while their troops fight each other. *Gwyddbwyll*, according to John Matthews, 'is a form of chess in which a central king with a handful of supporters strove to outwit a greater number of opposing warrior pieces.'[2] And this is what seems to be happening in the battle. Owein's troops are described as black ravens and it is not clear whether they really are birds or whether they represent his mother Morgan le Fey, who may have been linked to the Morrigan, a Celtic goddess whose emblem was the raven.

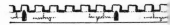

The battle rages one way and then the other, with various messengers exhorting the two chiefs to call off their side, at which the men, enigmatically, sometimes respond and sometimes keep playing. Much is made of the colours of the horses and the messengers, which are clearly significant. Arthur is called Emperor and wears a ring with a magic stone in it. Rhonabwy is told that simply by noticing the stone he will be able to remember the dream.

The whole story has an air of magic about it and is tantalizingly full of allusions, possibly of an alchemical nature. It looks back in style to Celtic riddle and fancy and captures the strongly mystical aspect of Arthur at that time.

Three further stories from the *Mabinogion* – *Owein*, *Peredur* and *Gereint and Enid* – are known as the Welsh Romances. These tales are also found among the French Romances (see below).

Geoffrey of Monmouth

Geoffrey of Monmouth was the Welsh or Breton author of the racy *History of the Kings of Britain*, written in Latin around 1136. He drew on

the works of Gildas, Bede and Nennius and on oral sources from Wales, Cornwall and Brittany. He also claimed to have used an ancient book written in the British language, but no other evidence of this exists.

Geoffrey's *History* consists of a patchwork of source material embroidered with a true storyteller's imagination. In it he sets out to trace a line of British monarchs from Brutus, grandson of Aeneas of Troy, claiming that Brutus escaped to Britain and colonized it, and that Arthur was descended from him. In writing the *History*, Geoffrey thus gave Britain a glorious and heroic past and, most of all, he gave England Arthur. In fact it was Geoffrey who gave the first full account of the origins and life of Arthur and exalted him to the status of King. He provided him with a powerful court at Caerleon-on-Usk and gave him Merlin as his advisor.

Geoffrey tells the story of Arthur's conception at Tintagel, of his crowning at the age of 15, and his subsequent battles against the Saxons, Picts and Scots. He tells of his marriage to Guinevere, of her infidelity with his nephew Mordred, who usurps his throne, and of the final battle at the River Camel in Cornwall, in which Mordred is killed. Finally he has Arthur being borne away, mortally wounded, to Avalon.

Typically Geoffrey makes high claims for Arthur, saying that he conquered Ireland, Iceland, Norway, Denmark and much of France, and even had designs on Rome. In making Arthur conqueror of France, Geoffrey was obviously seeking to please the new Norman dynasty. His *History* provided a heroic past for England to rival that of Charlemagne in France and, at the same time, it cast a welcome smear on the conquered Anglo-Saxons.

So Geoffrey was doing the Norman barons a favour by making historical what had previously been the stuff of myth and folklore. Of course, many of them had already heard tales of Arthur from the *conteurs* of northern France and Brittany. Such tales had reached Brittany when the Celts fled there to escape the Saxon invasions. These tales, however, were fanciful. By mixing supposed fact with fiction, Geoffrey laid the foundations on which the story of Arthur could flourish and move on into the sophistication of the French court. At the same time, he never lost sight of the story's Celtic

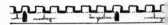

origins. For example, he made much of prophetic dreams and, most importantly, he introduced the druidic figure of Merlin.

WilliaM of MalMesBURY

Geoffrey's *History*, extremely popular in its day, has been dismissed by some sceptics as being mostly fiction. However, a more cautious historian, William of Malmesbury, a monk who carried out research in the library at Malmesbury Abbey and wrote his *Deeds of the English Kings* some ten years earlier, also concluded that Arthur was a historical figure:

> *This is that Arthur of whom the trifling of the Bretons talks such nonsense today; a man clearly worthy not to be dreamed of in false fables, but to be proclaimed in veracious histories, as one who long sustained his tottering country and gave the shattered minds of his fellow citizens an edge for war.*[3]

William was angry with Geoffrey for not being historically rigorous enough in his book, but it was Geoffrey's imaginative flair that captured the imagination of the people and ensured his success.

Wace

Geoffrey's *History* became the inspiration for all later literature concerning Arthur. The first to follow him was Wace, the Norman poet and cleric, with his *Roman de Brut (Romance of Brutus)* written in 1155 and dedicated to Eleanor of Aquitaine, wife of Henry II. It was the first of the French Romances, a poetic rendering of Geoffrey's story with some chivalric and romantic elements in it. Of Geoffrey's mixture of fact and fable he wisely observed: 'Truth stands hid in the trappings of a tale.'[4] Wace was responsible for introducing the Round Table, large enough to seat fifty knights, claiming that it came from British folklore.

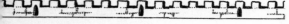

Layamon

At the end of the twelfth century, a priest from Worcestershire wrote an English version based mainly on Wace's *Brut*. His style was violent and bloodthirsty rather than romantic. He took the tale of the Round Table and made it the subject of a brawl among Arthur's company leading to bloodshed.

Layamon was also less sceptical than Wace about magic, and readily included the supernatural elements from Geoffrey of Monmouth's account, even adding some of his own. For example, he tells of a prophetic dream which Arthur has just before the last battle, in which he is sitting on the roof of his great hall while Modred (Mordred) hews down the posts and Guinevere pulls down the roof. He also adds the story of the boat with two beautiful women bearing away the dying Arthur. He shows, too, a firmer belief in the return of Arthur.

It was as a result of Layamon's work that Arthur, ironically, finally became a hero for the English, the very race that had been his chief foe.

Chrétien de Troyes

Chrétien was the most famous of the medieval romance writers. He was a French storyteller of the new Courtly Love fashion of the late twelfth century. He took the Arthurian tales that had come across to France with the Celts fleeing from the advancing Saxons, and recast them for the elegant court of Eleanor of Aquitaine, whose daughter Marie de Champagne was his patron.

His stories were written in verse, in the literary form of the *Romance* which was a long tale of chivalric adventure. The emphasis in his version of the tales is less on King Arthur as heroic warrior, and more on the chivalry of the knights – especially their relationship with women.

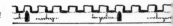

He wrote five romances in all. *Erec et Enide* and *Yvain* deal with the tension between love and chivalry within marriage. Another version of these stories is found in the *Mabinogion* – which was written at much the same time and therefore must have come from a similar source, presumably oral. But two further stories, *Cligés*, which was inspired by the story of Tristan and Iseult, and *Lancelot*, are not recorded elsewhere. So, not surprisingly, it would seem that Chrétien was responsible for introducing the theme of adulterous love – and especially the figure of Lancelot, the French Knight *par excellence*, whose affair with Guinevere rapidly became the central theme in the legends.

In order to foster the Courtly Love ideal, Chrétien went to great lengths to explain the actions of the knights, inventing honourable motives for them wherever possible. His version of the Arthurian tales changed their nature radically, making them more attractive to a female audience.

However, Chrétien finally went beyond the ideal of *amor* and *chivalrie*. He had already brought a strong Christian element to the stories with frequent mention of Church festivals, chapels and hermits, and in his last tale, *Perceval*, he introduced the idea of the spiritual quest. A more rudimentary version, *Peredur*, can be found in the *Mabinogion*, so, again, there must have been a common source, but it was Chrétien who made the story so compelling by introducing the enigmatic symbol of the Graal, or Grail, thought to mean a dish or platter. Tantalizingly his story remained unfinished at his death.

ROBERT DE BORON

After Chrétien's death several attempts were made to compose suitable endings for *Percival*, with varying success. Then in 1200 Robert de Boron wrote *Joseph of Arimathea*, a poetic trilogy which contained stories of Merlin, Lancelot and the Quest of the Grail. Robert de Boron was the first to Christianize the grail by linking it to Joseph of Arimathea and making it the cup of Christ. In Chrétien's story its origin was unknown.

The Vulgate Cycle

Between 1215 and 1235 an anonymous prose compilation of all the Arthurian stories was made in French, probably by a group of Cistercian monks. Known as the *Prose Lancelot* or the *Vulgate Cycle*, its scope is astonishingly wide. It deals with the origins of the Grail and includes all the chivalric adventures of Arthur's knights up to the death of Arthur. It is set out like a chronicle, giving the illusion of historical fact to the tales. It also interlaces the stories in order to create a feeling of continuity.

Disentangled, it gives five main stories: The Origin of the Grail, Merlin, Lancelot, The Grail Quest and The Death of Arthur. Some theological discussion is incorporated into it and some of the tales are recast in a Christian mould. For example, the tale of Merlin, though based on Geoffrey of Monmouth and Wace, shows Merlin finally at the mercy of Nimue, the wicked sorceress – which gives occasion for a sermon against the evils of women.

In contrast, there is an older tale of Merlin in which he simply becomes a mystical recluse, looked after by his sister (see Chapter 3). Nevertheless the theological bias tends to be mystical and concerned with inner journeying, which was a feature of Cistercian faith. So it was not entirely inconsistent with the enigmatic qualities of the Grail.

There are also some inspired additions. For example, the story of Lancelot contains a superb twist, that of the birth of Galahad sired by Lancelot on Elaine, the Grail Maiden, when she was enchanted to look like Lancelot's true love, Guinevere.

Malory

Although other important medieval works appeared, such as *Perlesvaus* and *Sir Gawain and the Green Knight*, the figure towering behind the Arthurian stories in the Middle Ages is undoubtedly Thomas Malory.

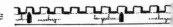

Malory wrote most of his famous work in Newgate gaol. He is thought to have been a Yorkist knight who served during the Wars of the Roses, possibly changing sides later on, and was tried for attempts of murder, robbery, rape, and cattle-stealing, serving a sentence during the 1460s. The terms of his imprisonment must have been fairly lenient because he seems to have had access to much source material. His main source, however, was the French *Vulgate Cycle*. He shortened the tales, cut out the rambling descriptions and the theological debates, and heightened the dramatic content. His style was colourful and immediate.

Malory wrote several books in an assorted chronological order. The first, *The Noble Tale of King Arthur and the Emperor Lucius*, deals with Arthur's military sortie into France, but he altered the route to fit that of Henry V. The second, *The Tale of King Arthur*, deals with Arthur's begetting, marriage, setting up of the Round Table, and the imprisonment of Merlin by Nimue. It also incorporates the sad story of Balin and Balan, the ill-fated brothers who killed each other unknowingly. The third book, *The Noble Tale of Sir Lancelot du Lac*, was an edited version of the *Vulgate* story. The fourth, *The Book of Gareth* (see Chapter 5), is a remarkable tale the source of which is unknown.

However, it is in his last two books that Malory's powers are at their height. *The Tale of Sir Lancelot and Queen Guinevere* is a vivid portrayal of the tormented Knight's love for his Queen and also for King Arthur. It is strongly pervaded by the feeling of doom which foreshadows the break-up of the Kingdom. Malory's final book contained the even stronger tale of Arthur's death.

The manuscript of this work came into the hands of the printer William Caxton fifteen years after Malory's death. Caxton edited it heavily and renamed it the *Morte d'Arthur* in an effort to make it one whole story. The final result, beautifully and dramatically written and streamlined, has become the main text for all subsequent writings and studies concerning the 'Matter of Britain' – the body of Arthurian legends.

application

The language of dreams

Dreams are treated with respect in the legends of King Arthur. All the writers down to Malory included and recounted them. The idea of the importance of dreams came from the Celts. In *The Dream of Rhonabwy* we see the Celtic custom of *imbas forosna* in which the bard or prophet would lay himself down on a bullhide and go to sleep surrounded by *awen*, or watchers. This ritual prepared him to receive a dream that would enlighten the whole community.

If we take any time to notice our dreams today, we tend to interpret them on an individual basis. Yet Jung has discovered that at a deep level we have access to a common symbolism located in the collective unconscious. It is important that we recognize and respect this. Placing a notebook and pen beside your bed will often provoke a vivid dream. Writing down the dream afterwards will help you to interpret it.

You may begin to notice how often the symbolism of your dream draws on the legends of our land. A shared cultural symbolism suggests a shared responsibility. Perhaps it is time to think more widely about the significance of dreams on a communal and cultural level, as the Celts did, as well as on a personal one.

3

MERLIN AND THE ROLE OF WIZARDRY

The Druidic Heritage

It is no accident that in the *Matter of Britain*, Arthur, the great hero warrior king, has an even greater magical figure standing behind him. Such a combination has an ancient pedigree. The Celtic kings were subject to the Druids, a priestly caste. Consisting of three orders – Bards, Ovates and Druids – they were poets, teachers, philosophers, seers, mages and judges, keepers of the history of the people and of ancient magical lore.

The Bards were poets. It was their job to recite genealogies and the histories of ancient places; they also praised the king and recorded battles. The Ovates were of a higher order: they were seers with strong prophetic powers. They also had a strong link with the natural world, possessing knowledge of herbs, animals and tree lore. They had shamanistic shape-changing abilities, being able to take on different forms, particularly of animals. They could also move easily between this world and the Otherworld – between the temporal and the spiritual.

The highest order was that of the Druids, priests and teachers with knowledge of science and philosophy, and, in particular, of astronomy and astrology. They were not just mystics; they also held political power, being judges and also presiding at coronations. Their central philosophical statement was 'to honour the gods, to do no evil and to practise courage'.

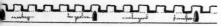

In the Arthurian legends the figure of Merlin conforms most to the Druidic order but there is evidence of his shamanistic prophetic and shape-changing abilities. An example of this is when he appears to Arthur first as a young boy and then as a very old man and prophesies the end of the kingdom, after Arthur has slept with his half-sister Morgause. In fact it is not surprising to find Merlin possessing these ancient abilities, for Merlin himself is a composite figure put together by Geoffrey of Monmouth from at least three different accounts, some of which are of extremely early origin.

Myrddin Wylt

Geoffrey first drew on an old Welsh legend of a sixth-century seer called Myrddin Wylt (Wild), who lived in the north-west of England and to whom people went for advice, as if to an oracle. He later became associated with Carmarthen in Wales.

According to this legend Myrddin was the court prophet of Gwenddoleu, a pagan king descended from Coel Hen (Old King Cole) who fought against a Christian king called Rhydderch Hael in the battle of Arfderydd, near Carlisle. When Gwenddoleu was defeated and killed in the battle, Myrddin was driven mad by grief at the death of his lord, and by horror at the slaughter – for which he felt some responsibility. He fled into the Caledonian woods and lived like a wildman for some 50 years. It was during this time of living so close to nature that he became like the old Ovates and acquired the gift of second sight.

He also had bardic skills and wrote long poems. For example there is an ancient Welsh poem of his about an apple tree where he says: 'While I was in my right mind I used to have at its foot/A fair wanton maiden, one slender and queenly.' Now he is lonely and grief-stricken, afflicted with madness and with *gwyllon*, spirits or ghosts, who haunt the woods.

In another poem he addresses his little pig, who seems to be his animal companion. In this poem he complains of the thinness of his

cloak and his grey hair, the lack of his lord, and of his gift of prophecy, which reveals the strife and disorder that is to come.

In all of this we can see the shadowy characteristics of the ancient shaman. These were that he lived close to the natural world, often accompanied by an animal; he had a period of initiatory madness, spoke with spirits and could prophesy, heal and cast out evil spirits. This legend, therefore, could contain the remnants of an ancient British shamanic tradition. Also, the pig was particularly associated with the Otherworld in Celtic belief and therefore seems an apt companion for Myrddin as Celtic shaman.

Myrddin's prophecies are found in other old Welsh poems such as the *Conversation of Myrddin and his Sister Gwendydd* composed in the magical triple-line form of the *englyn*. In it his sister calls him, 'my Llallogan Fyrddin, sage, prophet'. Llallogan is the Welsh version of Lailoken (see below).

Lailoken

A continuation of the story of Myrddin is found in the twelfth-century Scottish *Life of St Kentigern*. Geoffrey drew on this source as well for his *Life of Merlin*. In it Lailoken (Myrddin) has been rescued from his mad wanderings in the woods by St Kentigern and has been taken to the court of Rhydderch. He hates being back at court, even though it means being reunited with his wife. His attempts to escape result in his being imprisoned. He eventually secures his release by prophesying and performing the function of the Fool.

The Three Sardonic Laughs

A fool thrives on irony and there is something ancient and folkloric in the Lailoken story of the three sardonic laughs. The first was when he saw a leaf in a queen's hair, which showed that she had lain with a lover; the second was when he saw a beggar seated on

the ground and knew that buried treasure lay beneath him; the third was when he saw a man buying an expensive pair of shoes not knowing that he was destined to die within a day.

It is interesting that in the *Life of St Kentigern* a great effort is made to put the saint on the same footing as Lailoken. For example, the saint is shown taming the wild animals and even prophesying. This shows the struggle between the druids and the saints, the old priesthood and the new. In many of the saints' *Lives* dialogues and contests are depicted between the two.

However, there is a more tragic note in this particular tale, for the fooling of Lailoken ends when a voice from heaven pronounces: 'Lailoken, Lailoken, you alone will bear punishment'.[5] And Lailoken also prophesies his own threefold death. Later his death is reported: 'Pierced by a stake, suffering by stone and by water,/ Merlin is said to have met a triple death.'[6]

Ambrosius or Myrddin Emrys

By a bold stroke, Geoffrey combined Myrddin the Wild with a totally different character, that of Ambrosius, who appears in Nennius' account of Vortigern – the foolish British leader who brought in extra Saxons as mercenaries. This Ambrosius whom Geoffrey later calls Myrddin Emrys, is not to be confused with Ambrosius Aurelius, the Roman leader who was Arthur's predecessor in the fight against the Saxons.

Nennius' account is a strange one and involves the boy's supernatural powers, so perhaps this is why Geoffrey used it for his *History*. The story tells how Vortigern, fleeing from the Saxon mercenaries who have turned on him, attempts to construct a fortress at Dinas Emrys in Snowdonia, and is dismayed when it repeatedly collapses. He consults his magi, who tell him to sacrifice a fatherless young boy and sprinkle his blood on the foundations – an echo of an old Celtic ritual.

Eventually a boy is found whose mother is said to have been visited by an incubus. The boy, however, reveals by his druidic powers that there is a hollowed out stone beneath the foundations which contains warring red and white dragons. Vortigern has them dug up, whereupon they fly into the air and resume their fight. The boy then interprets this as the war between the Britons and the Saxons. The Saxons will have the upper hand for a while and then will be defeated by the Britons.

GEOFFREY'S MERLIN

In his version of this story Geoffrey says the boy was also called Merlin. (It has been conjectured that he deliberately changed the earlier Myrddin to Merlin to avoid the embarassing French word *merde*.) Geoffrey then has him prophesy the coming of Arthur as the 'boar of Cornwall' who will subdue the Saxons.

Inspired by an old Cornish legend, Geoffrey then tells the story of how Merlin enchants Uther Pendragon into the likeness of Gorlois, husband of the beautiful Igraine, so that he can gain entry to her windswept castle at Tintagel and sleep with her. In this way Merlin masterminds Arthur's conception, but this is the only role Geoffrey gives him in his *History*.

Later on, however, Geoffrey wrote a separate *Life of Merlin*. This was a private poem intended for a small circle of friends. In it he used much of the Myrddin Wylt material, which suggests that he discovered these sources after writing his *History*. He tried to equate the two Merlins but not very successfully as there was a gap of one hundred years between them. Nevertheless, thanks to Geoffrey, the Merlin of the later Romances has something of the historical wild Myrddin about him and it is this which makes him such a fascinating and complex character.

Merlin and the Devil

Robert de Boron gives us an intriguing though Christianized supernatural origin for the Magician. His poem *Merlin* appeared around 1200 as a sequel to his *Joseph of Arimathea*. It begins with an imaginative scene set in Hell, where demons are plotting to produce an anti-Christ who is part-human and part-devil and will have the gift of prophecy. A demon then visits a young girl and impregnates her while she is asleep. The girl tells her priest, who quickly purges her with holy water and the sign of the cross, blesses the child in her womb and imposes chastity on her. In this way the demon is outwitted but the child is able to retain his prophetic powers.

This story was an ingenious attempt to put a druidic figure into a Christian context, allowing Merlin to retain his supernatural powers while serving a Christian king. Otherwise the concept of Merlin would have posed problems for the Christian reader, who had a very different view of spirituality from that of the pagan Celt.

Celtic and Christian spiritual beliefs

In Celtic times there was no concept of good and evil as such. Instead the balance between good and evil, black and white, death and life, was easily understood and individual deities were understood to represent the two in one. For example, the Great Goddess who embodied nature also embodied the life and death principle and contained within her person the light and dark aspects of life. This idea was rejected by Christians for whom light and dark, good and evil, were split and had to have different impersonations. Under this new thinking the primitive wild man with strange prophetic powers came to be identified with the Devil.

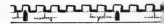

CERNUNNOS

The Christian concept of the Devil is also linked with the Celtic horned god Cernunnos, otherwise known as Lord of the Beasts because of his ability to tame wild animals and live among them. In his shamanistic wildman existence it can easily be seen that Merlin has links with him. In fact, there is a very suggestive episode in Geoffrey's *Life of Merlin* which shows him rejecting his wife Gwendoloene but then killing her new bridegroom by throwing the antlers of a stag at him.

In the story Merlin is said to rip the antlers off a stag's head but Nicolai Tolstoy has argued plausibly that he may have taken them from his own head, and that he could have been wearing an antlered helmet.[7] Also in many of the stories he is seen as a trickster, laughing at the situations his supernatural knowledge reveals.

MERLIN AND CHRIST

Although Merlin was linked through the tales of his fathering with the god Cernunnos or the Devil, through his mother, he was linked with Christ. Robert de Boron's story of Merlin's mother's innocence and impregnation by a supernatural being, coupled with her piety makes her a type of the Virgin Mary. Added to this is the strange prophecy from the Lailoken story, quoted above, which lays a general punishment on him. Then there is his own prophecy of his threefold, and therefore ritual, death.

THE ROLE OF THE FOOL

It seems that in these more ancient versions Merlin is symbolically a type of scapegoat. His portrayal as the fool also suggests this. The fool is characteristically a loner, living on the edge of society, childlike, but with the child's closeness to the unconscious. In this way he bears the burden of a wisdom beyond normal understanding. Yet he forms a bridge for mankind between the conscious and the unconscious, the human and the transcendent, between this world and the next. This is a painful place and a hard calling. It involves undergoing the danger of madness in order to perceive at a deeper level. The bearer of this knowledge sacrifices his life to attain a higher wisdom. He serves society in the deepest way possible but remains an outcast.

Robert de Boron's Merlin is a fool, trickster, shape-shifter and sorcerer, yet he uses his supernatural powers for the good of the realm. It is he who masterminds Arthur's becoming King, who contrives the test of the sword in the stone, who establishes the Round Table, and who sets in motion the strange, profound and esoteric quest for the Grail. It was de Boron, therefore, who took the great magician right into the story of Arthur and provided the complex and intriguing model for Malory's Merlin.

CƆERLIN ANĐ ThE GIANTS' ĐANCE

An intriguing story told by Geoffrey in his *History* demonstrates Merlin's druidic, astronomic and scientific skills and concerns the time when Merlin was adviser to Aurelius. Aurelius wanted to build a memorial to the 460 British warriors who were treacherously slain by the Saxons in Vortigern's time, and he asked Merlin for his advice. Merlin immediately suggested bringing the Giants' Dance from Ireland. This was made of magical stones for it was said that water used to wash the stones had the power to cure diseases.

Uther laughed at Merlin's suggestion because of the huge size of the stones, but Merlin insisted that he knew how to move them. Merlin then masterminded their removal, not by supernatural powers but by some ingenious engineering device that he had invented. In this way the stones were moved, so the legend goes, and stand as Stonehenge today.

Although it is not believed that the stones actually came from Ireland, it has certainly been proved that they came from the Preseli Mountains in Pembrokeshire and it is possible that this tale preserves an ancient folk-memory of their transportation.

The passing of Merlin

There are many stories concerning the passing of Merlin. The most famous comes originally from the *Vulgate Cycle* and shows him becoming pathetically in thrall to a beautiful woman who has been variously called Niniane, Nimue or Viviene, and is either a goddess, sorceress or damsel of the lake. In this version the besotted Merlin teaches his beautiful temptress all he knows of magic until she finally traps him in a cave or chamber by means of his own magic.

Although this has become the most famous story, it differs completely from earlier versions. For example, in his *Life of Merlin*, Geoffrey recounts how Merlin withdraws with his sister Ganeida into a vast observatory which she has constructed for him with seventy doors and windows, where they remain to this day, studying astronomy, philosophy and magic.

In an anonymous thirteenth-century work known as the *Didot Perceval*, Merlin is shown as surviving until after the last battle and then retreating to an *esplumoir*, a moulting cage used to collect the feathers of hawks. This could mean that he was caged and trapped or that he was shedding his feathers before entering a new existence. In shamanic tradition the image of a bird symbolized the soul.

Another early account says that Merlin gathered up the Thirteen Treasures of Britain and disappeared with them into his Glass House on Bardsey Island. Although a medieval manuscript contains a dubious list of them, the Thirteen Treasures are thought to come from very ancient sources and include such magical items as the Sword of Rhydderch, the Horn of Bran, the Cauldron of Dyrnwch, the Mantle of Arthur which gives invisibility, and the Chessboard of Gwenddolau in which the silver pieces move by themselves.

Then again, as we have seen, the Lailoken story suggests that Merlin underwent a ritual triple-death and became a scapegoat or punishment-bearer in the manner of Christ. In this respect many recent writers have seen parallels between Merlin and Lugh, the Celtic god of light, whose Welsh counterpart Lleu also underwent a ritual killing, shape-changed into an eagle and was revived to rule again.

With so many positive earlier accounts of Merlin's passing, it is surprising that he was given such a discreditable end by the writers of the *Vulgate Cycle*. Perhaps they wanted to combat the high claims being made for him. Certainly, for religious reasons, they wanted to demonstrate the evil power of magical or druidic women. Nevertheless, at another level, the story of Merlin's imprisonment could be symbolic of a shift from masculine to feminine magical power (see Chapter 8).

The older stories, however, provide a more appropriate end for him. It seems fitting that Merlin the mystic should retire to an Otherworldly resting place, retaining some guardianship of the land – especially as, according to oral tradition, Britain was once called *Clas Myrddin* (Merlin's Enclosure). It also seems appropriate that Merlin's passing should echo that of Arthur. For it is easy to see how their combined powers would be needed to secure the health of the land, with Arthur the active warrior, defending and cleansing it, and Merlin the seer, guarding its inner wisdom.

application

The wisdom of the fool

The Wise Fool is a profound concept. In the *Tarot* the Fool is a very powerful card to draw. It symbolizes the soul's quest for wisdom and perfection. The Fool is a loner who forsakes material possessions, preferring spiritual riches. His gifts are hard-won. He generally achieves spiritual knowledge after a period of madness and deprivation. He is often the lonely mediator for

society, speaking truths that society is unwilling to hear. The role of the Fool is a dangerous one. It can involve delusions and self-aggrandizement. Nevertheless there is a Wise Fool in each of us that must be listened to and respected.

The Fool is just one aspect of the Magician. The figure of Merlin embodies that of the Wise Man and Fool together. The Wise Man is an archetypal figure. He resembles that of the Druid. This figure is particularly powerful because he contains the masculine attributes of action and universal energy in combination with the feminine force of intuition. He is the repository of wisdom and experience issuing in magical energy.

VISUALIZATION: The WISE OLD MAN

Find a comfortable place where you can sit for five to ten minutes without being disturbed. Close your eyes and try to still your mind from the concerns of the day.

Imagine you are travelling along a path in a lightly wooded place. Shafts of sunlight strike through the trees and you are walking through bars of darkness and dappled light. The scent of wild garlic combined with other herbs gives a pungent woody aroma. Leaves tremble slightly in the air around you and insects and birds are your companions. After a while you see a pleasant glade ahead and decide you will sit down and rest in it. You find a bank of dried leaves and moss and lean against it. You open your backpack and have some refreshment. Afterwards you lie down in the leaves and close your eyes.

Immediately everything goes dark, and you see a flicker of light coming through the trees towards you. You are not afraid and after a while you see what it is. An old man holding up a lamp is proceeding slowly but deliberately towards your glade. Reaching it he puts down the lamp and looks about him. Seemingly oblivious of you he prepares a fire and places a mixture of herbs on it. The aroma is strong but sweet. It produces pictures in your mind.

First you see an animal. You are not sure in the smoke whether it is the Wise Old Man himself who has taken this shape. What animal do you see? You can ask it a question. When you have your answer you will find it changes shape. Now you see an image of someone you know. This could be someone who is alive today, or someone who has already died. They have a message for you. What is it? Now you see something natural. It could be a tree, a herb, a flower. This is your gift. What significance does it have for you? Does it link in any way with the other images?

After a while you wake up to find that the Wise Old Man and his fire and images have disappeared, as have the glade and the woodland. You are back in your present reality.

If you found the images difficult to understand, don't worry. Let them stay with you over the next few days and see if you gain an insight into your present situation from the memory of them. Also recognize that in dwelling on these visions you gain an awareness of the interconnection of all animate things. As if you yourself were a shape-shifter, you can enter into the spirit of animals, people and the natural world in your imagination.

4

CACIC ANO
SYCMBOLISCM

A great stone four square, like unto a marble stone, and in midst thereof was like an anvil of steel a foot on high, and therein stuck a fair sword naked by the point, and letters there were written in gold about the sword that said thus: Whoso pulleth out this sword of this stone and anvil is rightwise King born of all England.[8]

There are four main magical symbols at the heart of the Arthurian tradition, known as the four Hallows. These are the Sword, Spear, Stone and Cup. The origins of these are found in the four magical objects that the Celts believed were brought by the faery race, the Tuatha de Danaan when they conquered Ireland. The Celts linked the four objects symbolically with the four directions and the four elements.

- **The Stone of Destiny** The stone was the symbol of earth and was linked to the north. It is a feminine symbol. The magical Stone of Destiny, the *Lia Fail*, was the great crowning stone for the kings of Ireland because it would roar when the rightful monarch stood on it. Other large stones were used for swearing oaths. Standing stones and stone circles were infused with powerful earth energies and were connected with physical sensation and the healing power of the land.
- **The Spear of Lugh** The spear was the masculine symbol of fire and was linked to the south and to inspiration, energy and intuition. In Irish Celtic tradition it originally belonged to the god Lugh who, though multi-skilled, was especially associated with

smithcraft. This skill, which involved working with fire, was considered to have a magical dimension.

- **The Sword of Nuada** The sword was the symbol of air and was linked to the east. It was associated with the silver-handed god Nuada and with the wands of the Druids. It was a strong masculine symbol and denoted the cutting power of the word and of wisdom and intellect. In the hands of a king it could also show authority and justice.

- **The Cauldron of the Dagda** The cauldron or cup was a symbol of water and was linked to the west. It was a feminine symbol of feeling and emotion. It was associated with the Dagda, an early Irish god who possessed a magic cauldron of plenty. It was also a symbol of regeneration. Wells, springs and rivers were considered by the Celts to be the source of life and gateways to the Otherworld.

In the Arthurian tradition these four objects take on an enriched symbolism, the Sword of Nuada becoming Arthur's sword *Excalibur*, the Spear of Lugh the blood-dripping lance in the Grail legend, and the Cauldron of the Dagda the Grail itself. The *lia fail* becomes the stone in which Merlin sets the sword that only the true king can raise.

The sword in the stone

The concept of the 'sword in the stone' is a fascinating one because it combines two symbols. The sword is the masculine principle of intellect which has to be pulled from the feminine symbol of earth. Psychologically this indicates the separation of the male principle from the female, or the point in a hero's development when he has to separate from his mother and take on his own power. It also denotes the separation of the conscious from the unconscious. In the case of Arthur it is a huge moment in his life. He not only has to grow into his own manhood, but must also lay claim to his own wisdom and take on the role of kingship.

Excalibur

The sword is a dominating symbol in Arthurian legend. The magical sword Excalibur was given to Arthur by the Lady of the Lake. Again, this story contains a powerful combination of symbols, but this time featuring air and water. The masculine principle of wisdom and intellect has come up from the depths of the feminine element of water where it was charged with special magical properties.

Excalibur symbolically combines intellect with intuition, a powerful union of male and female attributes. This is emphasized by the fact that the sword and the scabbard are given together. When Arthur says he considers the sword more important than the scabbard, Merlin tells him the scabbard is ten times more magical because it protects the wearer from death.

The Lady of the Lake

The unnamed Lady of the Lake was a powerful faery woman who lived in a kingdom beneath the water. She also presided over several Damsels of the Lake, one of whom was Nimue, who enchanted Merlin. In Celtic belief the Ladies and Damsels were called *Morgans* and were seen as water deities residing in the Otherworld or Land of Youth, which was often depicted as an underwater island.

The Lady of the Lake gave Arthur the precious sword Excalibur with its life-preserving scabbard. She was also the foster-mother of Lancelot du Lac, who was brought up in her palace until she armed him and sent him to Arthur's court. She represents the feminine force of healing and renewal of life. The protective powers contained in the scabbard served Arthur until he was deceived by another faery woman, Morgan le Fey, whose name suggests that she, too, was originally a water deity.

The Dolorous Stroke

The spear is another mystical object in the Arthurian tradition. Associated with the wand, it carries with it connotations of a higher wisdom, such as the Druids possessed. In this respect, the spear is identified with the lance which drips blood and is carried in procession with the Holy Grail. In ancient ritual it could have been the male counterpart to that great femine symbol. It was also believed to represent the spear which pierced Christ's side on the cross.

At an earlier point in the Grail story, the knight Sir Balan, when fleeing weaponless from King Pelham, finds and picks up 'a marvellous spear strangely wrought.'[9] This has been identified with the Lance of Longinus with which Christ was pierced on the cross. With this spear Sir Balan deals King Pelham the Dolorous Stroke. King Pelham, later known as the Fisher King, suffers endlessly from this strange wound which afflicts both him and the land – which is linked to him symbolically.

The Grail

The magic cauldron of the Celts had always been a particularly potent symbol. As used by the Dagda it was able to produce unlimited quantities of food and also it was said that when dead heroes were placed inside it they returned to life. The cauldron was also traditionally associated with witches and black magic, but in the Arthurian tales it was transmuted into the Holy Grail, which made it the symbolic cup or vessel *par excellence*. Its ancient association with water and thus with the source of life made it the most exalted feminine symbol.

(DAGICAL FORESTS

In the Arthurian stories the questing knights are constantly shown
riding in and out of the realms of faerie. Such journeyings are
analogous with Otherworldly experiences which, in turn, can be
seen as spiritual or psychological tests. For example, many quests
necessitated going through a mysterious enchanted forest. Most of
the land at that time was covered in forest, and in legend traversing
these dark places was never straightforward.

The forest is an untamed place, a place of danger and freedom,
outside civilization. It is a place of hunting, lovemaking and
antiquity – the wild haunt of primitive man, also of Druids and
treelore. In Arthurian legend forests were populated by strange
beings, otherworldly creatures – enchanters, witches, sorcerers,
giants, dragons, those who had been changed into another shape
and were seeking redress, mythical creatures who might appear and
disappear at will. The adventurous knight would have to brave not
only physical dangers which tested his prowess, but also the
dangers of the unknown. The forest was a place of chaos, an
irrational feminine place which the masculine light of the sun could
hardly penetrate, a land of dreams.

Psychologically the forest corresponds to the dark, irrational realm
of the unconscious. In the legends it is usual for a knight to make
such a quest alone. This is because he is journeying into an aspect
of himself that he must learn to conquer. The damsels, towers and
beasts that he meets are all symbols within his own psyche. The
damsel who offers him romantic love is a distraction luring him into
an unreal dreamworld. The castle often symbolizes imprisonment,
the giant embodies brute forces, and the dragon, destructiveness. All
these untamed elements lie within the knight's psyche and must be
mastered if he is to attain his higher self.

OWAIN OR THE COUNTESS OF THE FOUNTAIN

Broceliande in Brittany was the epitome of magical forests. It was the setting for *Owain*, a tale from the *Mabinogion*, and also for Chrétien de Troyes' *Yvain*. The former tells how Owain goes into the forest deliberately to seek an extraordinary adventure. He is told who he has to meet on his quest and it is easy to see that these beings are initiatory helpers and testers. The first is a huge black man with one foot and one eye in the middle of his forehead, who carries an immense iron spear. He has power over the wild animals so that they bow down to him. He is reminiscent of Cernunnos, the Celtic god of the beasts. The single eye in his forehead is like the eye of knowing, or second-sight, which is located in the brow. His spear is like a Druid's hazel wand.

It is interesting that Owain meets such a figure at the threshold of his adventure into the unknown. In his quest Owain needs great physical strength and it seems that the animal kingdom is ready to help him. The black giant represents both intuition and a mastered strength. He is an intermediary between man and the forces of nature and Owain can derive the power of physical might from him as well as the power of intuition which will take him from one world to another.

Next Owain has to go to the sacred spring (identified with the Fountain of Barendon). This is a very potent place. As we have seen, the Celts considered wells and springs to be the source of life, and gateways to the Otherworld. They were connected to female deities. Owain is given instructions to enable him to activate the great force within the spring. He must collect water from the fountain in a silver bowl and then pour it onto a great stone nearby. As soon as he does this there arises a terrible storm which is severe enough to threaten his life. When it finally abates he hears a great singing of birds. Birds and birdsong are a marked feature of Celtic descriptions of the Otherworld, so this is a clear indication that he is now in another realm.

Immediately after this a noise of groaning through the valley announces the entrance of an unknown black knight with whom he must fight. Owain kills the knight and marries his lady, who is the Countess of the Fountain. Here we see the Celtic motif of the aged king being overcome by the younger man, who claims the goddess and ensures the fertility of the land. This derives from the triumph of spring over winter and, ultimately, the triumph of life over death (see Chapter 1).

The fact that Owain later forgets about his marriage also strongly suggests that this was an Otherworldly experience which fades from his memory when he returns to the 'real' world. However, when he is reminded of his love and realizes he has lost her, he goes mad. When he recovers from his madness he goes through further trials of courage but is accompanied by a lion who helps him. The story, as well as being about healthy relationship with the female, seems to suggest that a good relationship with the animal kingdom is also important in gaining the riches of the Otherworld.

The king

The role of the king has been of critical importance from earliest times. The king represented the apex of the ordered world. As such he was the earthly reflection of the supreme divinity. A good king ensured stability and prosperity. The ritual renewal of the king was of great importance in Celtic mythology, because the health of the land depended on him. If he could not be regenerated then the sun would not return and if he became impotent then the land would become barren.

In psychological terms he is also linked to the sun as the masculine conscious ego. He symbolizes rationality; his power is that of the hero and he champions law, order and justice. A bringer of light into dark places, he fights with the dark forces of the unconscious in order to discover the potential within his own conscious ego. Ideally he contains within himself the attributes of both king and wise man. In the case of Arthur this role was shared with Merlin.

The Round Table

The famous Round Table of Arthur's court is also an important symbol. Linked to the king it represents cosmic law or the ordered universe. As a circle it represents wholeness and perfection and the wheel of life. It not only stands for the round earth but also mirrors the heavens above with its stars and planets. It is a type of mandala and suggests a map of the entire cosmos. Astrological divisions, and divisions of time, are also associated with it. Tennyson, in *Morte D'Arthur*, captivated its importance in two poignant lines:

> *But now the whole round table is dissolved*
> *Which was an image of the mighty world.*

Merlin's Round Table was set up as a place of meeting and council, with a designated place for each knight. The circle was incomplete while the *Siege Perilous* (Dangerous Seat) remained unoccupied waiting for the perfect knight to claim his place and complete the table before setting off to attain the highest quest, that of the Holy Grail.

The Round Table at Winchester.

The white hart

This is a fabulous beast that periodically bursts through the court of Arthur and provokes a quest or ritual hunt. In Chrétien de Troyes' story it is captured by Arthur, who brings the head back to court. Gawain is not happy about the hunt because traditionally the bearer of the white hart's head must bestow both the head, and a kiss, on the most beautiful woman at court. Invariably this custom led to strife. In this version the ritual hunt is linked to the love story of *Erec and Enide*, in which Enide provokes her husband into resuming his heroic career (see Chapter 8).

In another tale, the white hart dashes through Arthur's court at his wedding feast and is pursued by Gawain, who cuts off its head just before accidentally cutting off the head of a lady – for which unchivalrous deed he has to do a form of penance for the rest of his life (see Chapter 5).

The white hart is a feminine symbol of challenge, linked to the Goddess and denoting the transforming power of love. By bursting through the ordered court, the hart creates havoc and provokes change. Its white colour represents a spiritual quest but spiritual fulfilment can only be obtained after severe testing.

Castles

Castles contain little worlds within themselves. Surrounded by moats and battlements, they symbolize a Celtic Otherworldly realm which can only be reached by crossing water. As such they link with the Otherworld islands of Celtic mythology and, like them, can be timeless. The enchanted garden is also such a place, as is the walled town. Often questing knights, having defeated the defending knight, encounter mysteries of a feminine kind within the castle or garden where they can become imprisoned, enchanted by a spell. Usually they have to languish there until released by an outside agent, for knightly prowess alone is not equal to such Otherworldly powers.

Lancelot, however, successfully rescues Guinevere from her Otherworldly island where she has been taken by Melvas (or Meleagant), King of the Summer lands.

Jewels from the East

The obligation laid on knights to go on Crusades gave rise to a sudden, powerful contact with the east. Magical images borrowed from the Orient could happily be blended with that of the Celts to produce an even more exotic array of strange talismans, magic potions, alluring maidens, rich palaces and enchanted gardens. The importance of symbolic language was enhanced by this cross-fertilization and it is thought that Eastern mysticism, especially in the veiled symbolism of its love-poetry, was partly responsible for the rise of the courtly and chivalrous ideals of Arthurian knighthood.

APPLICATION

Recognizing the fourfold divisions

Set up a square table and place on it four objects to represent the four Hallows of stone, spear, sword and cup. Make sure they face the correct directions of north, south, east and west. Find other objects to add to them that symbolize the four elements, earth, fire, air and water. Place a candle in the middle of the table and light it. Use the table as a focus for your meditation. Become aware of the interconnection of the four symbolic objects, the four directions and the four elements.

If you prefer you can use Tarot cards or ordinary playing cards. The Pentacles or Diamonds symbolize the earth and stone. The Wands become Clubs and symbolize fire and the spear. The Swords or Spades correspond to air, and the Cups or Hearts symbolize water. These four symbols also relate to Jung's four functions of the psyche: sensation, intellect, intuition and emotion. Most people are less adept in one area and their task is to develop this in order to achieve a balanced psyche. If you keep finding yourself in a particular type of difficult situation or if you attract partners with opposing strengths to your own, it could be that you are being challenged to work on that area in yourself.

5 CHIVALRY

The word chivalry came from the French *chevalier*, or *horseman*. The concept became a feature of the Arthurian tradition when it crossed the Channel into France. It was built on the heroic ideal present in the stories from Celtic times. The concept of Courtly Love, as expressed in the poetry of the troubadours, became strongly linked to that of chivalry, particularly in the Romances of Chrétien de Troyes. However, it is important to make a distinction between the two ideologies.

In his *Morte D'Arthur* Malory gives a list of chivalrous ideals:

> ... then the King stablished all his knights ... and charged them never to do outrageousity nor murder, and always to flee treason; also by no mean to be cruel, but to give mercy unto him that asketh mercy, upon pain of forfeiture of their worship and lordship of King Arthur for evermore; and always to do ladies, damosels, and gentlewomen succour, upon pain of death. Also, that no man take no battles in a wrongful quarrel for no law, ne for no world's goods. Unto this were all the knights sworn of the Table Round, both old and young. And every year they were sworn at the High Feast of Pentecost[10]

The chivalric code consisted of qualities and virtues such as piety, honour, courage, courtesy and loyalty. These were inspired by three main ideals: the heroic ideal of the old Celtic epics, the service of the Christian faith, and the service of women. Courage and bravery in the field were still important, but now, thanks to French cultural influence, they had to be tempered with elegant manners and refinement. Christian virtues were also of great importance and all knights were expected to take part in the Crusades.

Chrétien de Troyes

In Chrétien's tales both chivalry and Courtly Love are of equal importance. Often they are combined, but occasionally a knight is torn between the two. An example is Lancelot's dilemma in having to choose between giving mercy to a vanquished foe, or beheading him to please the lady the foe has wronged:

> He wants to do what both girl and man ask. Generosity and Pity bid him do what each wants, for he was generous and compassionate. But if the girl carries off the head, then Pity is defeated and slain; and if she does not take it as her own, then Generosity is vanquished. This is the bondage and plight in which he is held by Pity and Generosity, tormented and afflicted by each.[11]

Lancelot is torn between a rule of Courtly Love, to give the lady what she asks, and a rule of chivalry, to show mercy to a vanquished enemy who pleads for it. But Lancelot must keep both rules, so Chrétien contrives an ingenious solution in which Lancelot shows mercy by offering the man a further fight. When he loses, he cuts off his head and gives it to the girl.

The hero within

Of course, the equitable outcome of this is dependent on Lancelot's fighting prowess. The function of knights in the Middle Ages was to defend the realm by keeping the peace and righting wrongs. This was also the pledge of the 'noble fellowship of the Round Table' in the Arthurian stories. But the nature of their heroism became more complex in French hands.

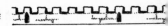

Whereas the Celtic Arthur was chiefly renowned as a hero in his own right, the chivalrous Arthur of the French Romances demonstrated less personal prowess, becoming more of a figurehead around which the actions of his knights revolved. This meant, too, that in most of the tales, knights went on quests alone. Their quests also became more complex and psychological, demonstrating that the chivalric ideal applied to both the outer and inner hero.

Individual quests were seen as opportunities for learning and self-development. This is made clear by the fact that the court acted as judge after a knight returned from a quest, assessing his actions and ordering his future behaviour. For example, after Gawain accidentally kills a woman who throws herself on the knight he is about to slay, he is required by Merlin to give an account of his adventure. He has to explain why he showed the knight no mercy and why he slew the lady. He is found guilty on both counts and is required by ordinance of the Queen to be courteous to women and undertake their causes, and to show mercy to those knights who ask it of him, for the rest of his life.

The knight riding alone, therefore, was not only braving dangers to the realm but was also riding out to face himself. As discussed in the previous chapter, symbolically the landscapes of the quests represented aspects of an inner journey. In undertaking a supernatural quest the knight was seeking danger for its own sake because it was impossible to calculate the risks involved. Seeking danger for its own sake meant showing prowess whatever might happen. This was the means by which a knight could discover his finer self. That this was his goal was made clear in the chivalric Romance of King Horn, who rode out on his first quest declaring:

> ... I must ride forth to prove my might;
> Must conquer hardships, and my own worse self ...[12]

Gareth and Lynet

A tale which involves the hero setting out to find himself by first deliberately obscuring his identity is that of *Gareth and Lynet*, also entitled *The Fair Unknown*. It tells how the hero Gareth arrives at Arthur's court and hides his noble breeding, humbly asking to be given food and lodging for a year. Mocked by Sir Kay and dubbed Beaumains ('Beautiful Hands'), he takes on the job of kitchen boy. He has, however, already secured two boons from Arthur. Firstly, that after a year he should be knighted by Lancelot and secondly, that he should be sent on a worthy errand. When the time comes Lancelot knights him and discovers that he is Arthur's nephew and brother to Sir Gawain, but promises to keep this secret. So when the haughty Lynet seeks Arthur's help to free her imprisoned sister, she is appalled when, instead of one of the more noble knights, the unknown 'knight of the kitchen' is given the task.

Beaumains sets off with Lynet and vanquishes several knights, including Sir Kay. Lynet treats him with contempt, claiming that he has simply been fortunate. His tests increase and he faces first the Black Knight, whom he kills, and then this knight's three brothers, the Blue, Green and Red knights, whom he pardons at the request of Lynet. They each promise to serve him with an increasing number of men.

Despite all this Lynet still scorns him. In return, he treats her with the utmost respect and vows that however badly she treats him, he will continue to follow her. Then, just before he meets his next challenger, Sir Persant of Inde, Lynet abruptly changes her attitude, saying that he must be born of noble blood: 'for so foul ne shamefully did never woman rule a knight as I have done you, and ever courteously ye have suffered me, and that came never but of a gentle blood.'[13] This gives Beaumains sufficient heart to win against Sir Persant and he finally reaches the Perilous Castle where Dame Lyonesse is held captive. Seeing her beautiful face at the window inspires him to conquer her captor, the Knight of the Red Launds.

Hoping to enjoy the love of Dame Lyonesse at last, he is dismayed when she sets him further tests. Then, after she has capitulated enough to come secretly to his bed and he is about to make love to her, her sister Lynet sends in a magical knight who wounds him in the thigh. Gareth kills him but Lynet magically restores him to life. This happens on two occasions. Finally Gareth organizes a huge tournament. Dame Lyonesse gives him a magic ring which obscures

his colours so that he will not be recognized and which also prevents his blood being shed. He wins the day both with and without the protection of the ring, and finally marries her.

In an earlier version of the story entitled *The Fair Unknown*, Gareth's mother is a faery, so there is genuine mystery about his parentage. Lynet is also a faery and at first Gareth falls in love with her, but then switches his affections to the lady he rescues.

In this story the female figures are the helpers and agents in Gareth's quest to find his identity. Lynet's disdain spurs him on to braver and braver feats. The knights he conquers are all brothers and each wears a different colour. They form a pattern of related aspects of his persona that have to be subdued. Each conquest wins him a greater retinue of men at his service. Lynet changes her strategy to that of encouragement when he needs further strengthening and then, in his finest hour, he is inspired by his future love, the Dame Lyonesse.

So far, he has proved himself in courage and in courtesy. Now he has to tame his lust, and the women alternate in setting this test. At the end he triumphs at a Great Tournament which is attended by all the characters in his life, which represent characteristics in his psyche. He moves among them in glittering, shifting colours until at last, having triumphed over every adversity, his true nature is revealed and he can wed his Lady.

Medieval knights and knighthood

The concepts of heroism and chivalry captured the imagination of medieval society. Because the Arthurian tales were recast in a contemporary setting, these concepts were, as far as possible, adopted by real-life knights.

In the eleventh century the creation of a knight involved a strict training. A young boy was sent away to another household to serve as a page and then as an esquire until finally attaining the golden spurs, the symbol of knighthood. The ceremonial required for the actual knighting was strongly religious. The night before being admitted to his order the candidate would take a ritual bath and then hold vigil, meditating throughout the night in a chapel. Then he would take confession and Holy Communion before being dubbed a knight by the flat of the sword on each shoulder.

Fully fledged knights were usually aristocrats who owned and ran their own estates and were responsible for keeping order and administering justice. Knighthood was a privilege confined to the aristocratic classes and became more exclusive as time went on. By the thirteenth century it was limited to the top ranks of aristocracy.

heraldry

The chivalric spirit also found expression in heraldry. This began as a means of identification but soon grew in decoration and formality and became an art in itself. Shields were later quartered in order to show family connections, genealogies and intermarriages. Shield shapes varied from kite-shaped to square with a notch on the side for resting the lance.

The heraldic system became formalized and acquired its own terminology. Colours were given names such as *gules* (red), *azure* (blue), *argent* (white), *or* (yellow), *sable* (black), *purpure* (purple), and *vert* (green). The position of animals was also stylized: for example *statant* (standing), *courant* (running), *trippant* (walking), *rampant* (rearing up with one hind leg on the ground), *salient* (rearing up with both hind legs on the ground), and *attired* (antlered). The animals most usually depicted were either fabulous or ferocious, such as unicorns, dragons, griffins, lions, tigers and boars.

Arthur and his knights were endowed with heraldic emblems. Nennius' description of Arthur carrying the image of the Virgin Mary 'on his shoulders', was taken as meaning 'on his shield' because the Welsh words *ysgwydd* and *ysgwyd* are almost identical. Arthur's shield, therefore, consisted of a white cross with the figure of the Virgin and Child, and three crowns, sometimes silver on blue, or otherwise gold on red. Lancelot's shield was generally white with

between one and three dark red bands. Sometimes a heart was added. Gawain's symbol was a pentangle, Galahad's a red cross on either a white or gold background. Tristan's emblem was a lion or a boar.

Crests also became fashionable towards the end of the medieval period. They were made of wood or boiled leather and bore the personal badge or device of the knight as opposed to the general family one. They were often very heavy but were still considered worth wearing.

ARMOUR

Although Arthurian knights are often depicted wearing plate armour, this appeared only in the fourteenth century. Medieval knights wore chain mail, which was an eastern invention. It comprised a coat or *hauberk*, leggings (*chausses*), hood (*ventail*), and mufflers or gloves. Underneath it was a padded jacket made of cotton, wool (*fustian*) or leather. Knights carried a wooden shield strengthened with metal bands. Such armour was light and flexible, weighing only about 60 pounds (27 kilos). The French romances tell of knights leaping from the ground into the saddle! The idea of knights being winched onto their horses is a Victorian fallacy. When plate mail came in, mostly to combat the faster crossbow, it was still fairly flexible, although for tournaments a heavier version was used with the crest often weighing as much as 20 pounds (9 kilos).

TOURNAMENTS

In medieval times tournaments became very fashionable and were based on the model provided by the legends. They consisted of one-to-one jousting or group *tourneys* using blunt weapons. Typically these would be swords or lances if fighting on horseback, and maces or axes if on foot. Tournaments were governed by strict rules and prizes were awarded, such as horses and armour. Ladies' favours such as gloves or sleeves were worn into combat.

Arthur's shield.

Henri, husband of Marie de Champagne, was a great supporter of tournaments in France, while in England Henry II banned them due to their being unruly. They were also condemned time and time again by the Catholic Church for being Godless and violent. However, they continued in defiance of such rulings. By the thirteenth century they had become a more limited contest relying on well-developed technical skills.

The last great tournament, The Field of the Cloth of Gold, was held by Henry VIII wearing a suit of golden armour: he proved himself a skilful fighter. Elizabeth I treated the tournament as a courtly amusement, using old-fashioned costumes and rules.

The Crusades

The Crusades provided a great opportunity for putting the chivalric concepts into practice. This opportunity was particularly relished by Richard the Lionheart, who even christened his sword Excalibur. Chivalry combined with spirituality was the inspiration behind the Crusades in which Christian knights took up arms against the Muslims in Palestine. The First Crusade was instigated by Pope Urban II at the Council of Clermont in 1095. It ended successfully with the conquest of Jerusalem in 1099.

The Second Crusade was inspired by the preaching of St Bernard of Clairvaux, but it was a disaster. There followed seven more Crusades, including the appalling Children's Crusade, but apart from a three-year truce, which allowed Christians access to Jerusalem, they achieved little.

Gawain and the role of the hero

Gawain was originally called *Gwalchmai* – Hawk of May. He was Arthur's nephew and his prime champion, being next in line to the throne through the Celtic system of succession. He was also the most courteous of knights and prime champion of women. Before Lancelot entered the story, there was no one to touch him for valour and chivalry. In the later stories he and Lancelot seem to form a pair. They love each other dearly and then end up trying to fight each other to the death, after Lancelot has mistakenly killed two of Gawain's brothers.

In this battle, Lancelot learns Gawain's secret which is that his power increases threefold between the hours of nine and noon, when the sun is at its highest. This suggests that originally Gawain was identified with a Celtic solar deity. Like earlier Celtic heroes, he is associated with a particular horse: his is called *Gringalet*. There is another curious detail given about him which is that he loves all fruit, particularly apples and pears.

Gawain is Arthur's closest companion, and is at times almost interchangeable with him. It is he who on behalf of Arthur, marries and kisses the Loathly Lady, the type of Celtic *Cailleach* who represents Sovereignty. This demonstrates his kingly qualities. Even after his death he does not quite disappear from the story. He appears to Arthur in a dream and warns him against engaging with Mordred in the Last Battle.

While being the exemplary hero, Gawain is still guilty of rash judgement. His insistence on fighting Lancelot to the death – for which he later apologizes, is of a piece with the rashness displayed throughout the legends by knights who are so keen to demonstrate their prowess that they forget to find out the identity of their opponent. On many occasions they discover that they have nearly killed a trusted friend, an honoured companion, or even the King himself because they did not take the time to enquire who they were. The saddest tale is of the two brothers Balin and Balan, who killed each other in this way. The lesson is that the role of the hero requires discrimination as much as prowess.

Symbolically the hero is linked with the king and, like him, is identified with the sun. Gawain's strength was directly connected with the sun. The sun is the ultimate symbol of consciousness and it is the role of the hero to bring unconscious forces into the light of

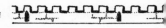

day in order to deal with them. He has to fight dragons and monsters and rescue maidens and treasures. His most difficult tasks are to relate to the maiden and to bring back the treasures, which are located in the unconscious. He is usually equipped with magical weapons which correspond to inner gifts or talents which he must utilize in order to succeed.

APPLICATION

The hero within

Everyone, whether male or female, has monsters and dragons to combat. These can begin as vague fears. The task of the hero within is to track these down and confront them. Common fears might include the fear of failure or of loneliness. Also fear of other people or of authority, or fear of the opposite sex. Part of the process involves recognizing and developing individual talents and strengths. These are the talismans such as rings and swords given to the hero by the faery helpers. It is important to allow yourself to be challenged in order to achieve self-mastery and self-development, but at the same time you need to discriminate between helpful and rash challenges.

6 COURTLY LOVE

*My commitment to Love will never be broken by any provocation
or hostility towards him on my part. Now let Love do what he
will with me, as he should with one who belongs to him, for I'm
content and wish it so and never want this sickness to leave me.*[14]

So declares the Greek youth Alexander, who is sickening of love
for Soredamors, the maiden with the golden hair. The words are
put into his mouth by Chrétien de Troyes in the opening pages of his
Romance, *Cligés*. By making Love into a divinity he is copying Ovid,
who in his erotic love poetry jokingly suggested that Eros should be
obeyed absolutely and without question like a general in battle:

*Every lover's on active service, my friend, active service, believe me,
    And Cupid has his headquarters in the field.
Fighting and love-making belong to the same age-group -
    In bed as in war, old men are out of place.
A commander looks to his troops for gallant conduct,
    A mistress expects no less.
Soldier and lover both keep night-long vigil,
    Lying rough outside their captain's (or lady's) door.
The military life brings long route-marches – but just let his mistress
    Be somewhere ahead, and the lover too
Will trudge on for ever, scale mountains, ford swollen rivers,
    Thrust his way through deep snow.*[15]

Although Ovid was being ironic, it seems that his idea of having
strict rules of behaviour in seduction was taken literally and became
the basis of an ideal code of conduct in matters of love. This ideal

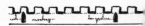

also became linked with the concept of chivalry exemplified in the tales of Arthur. At the same time the troubadour poets of the Languedoc area in southern France began writing their Courtly Love lyrics.

But why should this elevation of romantic love have suddenly appeared so forcefully? No one knows for sure but several theories have been put forward, some of which are social and others religious. For example, there was a mass exodus of knights going away on Crusade which meant that their wives were left to run the great households. This had several ramifications. Firstly, the wives were free to choose their own entertainment and would no doubt have preferred tales of love to tales of heroism. Secondly, with the knights abroad, the court minstrels would have been the only men around and it is easy to see how love affairs and infatuations might arise between these minstrels and their highborn Ladies chastity belts not withstanding.

There was also a strong dissenting religious movement at this time, that of Catharism, which, because of its popularity, was forced to go underground to escape persecution. It may have been inspired by a similar movement in the East, which was also under persecution. The influence these two religious ideologies may have had in terms of Courtly Love will be examined later in this chapter.

ELEANOR OF AQUITAINE

Eleanor of Aquitaine, Queen of France, then of England, but also self-styled queen of Love, was enormously important in terms of Courtly Love because she actually put into practice the tenets of this 'faith'. At a young age she was married to Louis VII. Fifteen years later the 19-year-old Henry II visited the court and fell in love with her. They had an affair and she became pregnant with his child. Louis divorced her and she married Henry in 1152. (Richard the Lionheart was their third child.)

Eleanor presided over a glittering court in the balmy climate of southern France which was attended by troubadours who praised her in their amorous verses and where she lived out the new romantic and courtly ideal. Her daughter by Louis, Marie de Champagne, also held court with her and became Chrétien de Troyes' patron.

The rules of Courtly Love

In 1185 Andreas Capellanus wrote a treatise on love for Marie de Champagne called *De Arte Honeste Amande* (On the Art of True Loving). It was a legal and theological treatise inspired by Ovid, and included 31 laws of Love, analogous to the Ten Commandments of the Christian faith. It became the basis of the elaborate code called *Fin' Amors* which was developed by the troubadours in their poetry.

The gist of these rules was that love was an exalted and religious feeling. The woman, as object of this feeling, was a superior being who could only be approached with reverence. The dynamic force of love had to be suffered like a sickness, all-consuming to the lover. The lover also had to become the servant of his lady and had to prove himself noble and faithful. The relationship was similar to the old feudal one between lord and vassal. In fact, the troubadours called the lady *midon* or 'my lord'.

The lady, being so elevated, was difficult to obtain, and her lover had to undergo severe hardships in order to win her. Such rules could only really relate to extramarital relationships: a married man regarded his wife as his subordinate, and marriage was largely a contract based on property.

Troubadours

Troubadours were the minstrels or poet-musicians of Provence and the Languedoc area of southern France in the twelfth and thirteenth centuries. The *trouvères* were their counterparts in northern France who tended to compose narrative songs. The troubadour poems

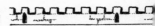

were mainly concerned with love and the courtly ideal. Both groups wrote their lyrics in the vernacular, breaking away from the use of Latin.

Much of the music composed by these performers has been lost. In fact, more than two thousand troubadour songs have survived but less than three hundred melodies. Of these only the notation has been recorded: the rhythm probably depended on poetic metre, or was memorized. They performed their lyrical poems to the harp, viele (fiddle), or an early type of lute. There were strict forms such as the *canso* (verse song), *tenso* (dialogue or debate), *planh* (complaint), *alba* and *serena* (morning and evening song). Many of the troubadours were noblemen rather than wandering minstrels, and they performed at the great houses of the aristocracy.

The earliest known troubadour was Guillaume of Aquitaine (1071–1127), grandfather of Eleanor. Other famous troubadours include Bertran de Born, Jaufrè Rudel and Bernard de Ventadour. Of these, Bernard was perhaps the most accomplished. His writing is vivid and immediate as can be seen in these two verses from *Can vei la Lauzeta*:

> *When I behold the lark arise*
> *with wings of gold for heaven's height,*
> *to drop at last from flooded skies,*
> *lost in its fullness of delight,*
> *such sweetness spreads upon the day*
> *I envy those who share the glee.*
> *My heart's so filled with love's dismay*
> *I wait its breaking suddenly.*
>
> *I thought in love's ways I was wise,*
> *yet little do I know aright.*
> *I praised a woman as love's prize*
> *and she gives nothing to requite.*
> *My heart, my life she took in theft,*
> *she took the world away from me,*
> *and now my plundered self is left*
> *only desire and misery.*[16]

The Cathars and the Divine Feminine

By the time the Arthurian Romances were being rewritten and embroidered, Christianity had become the recognized religion, and the Great Mother – venerated by the Celts, had long ago been replaced by the Father God. But the Arthurian legends with their age-old concept of chivalry, had always acknowledged the special place of women. When Christianity became increasingly patriarchal, therefore, the legends provided a refuge for the forgotten element of the Divine Feminine, whose flame had been kept alive by certain early Christian cults or groups.

One such group were called *Gnostics*, from the word *gnosis*, meaning 'inner knowing'. They believed in a mystical aspect of the Godhead, which they saw as the feminine principle which had been erroneously left out of the Godhead.

The recently discovered *Gnostic Gospels* are early Christian writings in which the person of the Holy Spirit in the Trinity seems to have been female. The idea, set out in St John's Gospel, of the Word which was 'in the beginning' and 'with God' links with the ancient Greek concept of Sophia, the female spirit of wisdom.

When, therefore, the Church of Rome finally hammered out its theology and came up with an orthodox set of beliefs, it rejected the Gnostic approach as heretical. But the Gnostics continued to practise their faith. One sect became known as the Cathars, or Albigensians because they lived near the town of Albi in the Languedoc area of southern France. This area was notable for its tolerance.

Although aware of the Church's disapproval of them, the Cathars considered themselves to be Christians. In fact they thought their faith was a particularly pure form of Christianity. They were critical of the Church of Rome because of the monopoly it seemed to have on Christianity. The Cathars believed that through mystical awareness anyone could learn new aspects of spiritual truth – which meant they rejected the idea that Christians needed instruction from the Church. In fact, they began to scorn the hierarchy of the Church, along with its patriarchal nature, considering that it was becoming corrupted by power and riches.

Because the Cathars were so popular, the Church became alarmed and began to hunt them down in an attempt to stamp out their heretical views. From 1204 onwards Simon de Montfort led obsessive and brutal attacks against them. Whole towns sympathetic to them were massacred, and individual Cathar leaders or *Parfaits* were incarcerated in the castle dungeons at Carcasonne. In 1244, more than two hundred devotees were burned in a field below Monteségur, now called the 'Field of the Burned'.

The Veiled Idea

At the same time, participation in the Crusades meant that the knights came in contact with Eastern culture and, in particular, with Arabic mystical poetry, which was set to music and performed by Saracen *jongleurs*. Some of these Moorish jongleurs travelled to the courts of France, England and Sicily. Their songs were erotic as well as mystical. In them the woman was exalted as an object of love but was understood to represent the Veiled Idea of the Divine Mystery.

Official Islam had the same rigid attitude towards religious orthodoxy as the Roman Catholic Church in the West, and ruthlessly opposed any mystical or experiential idea of the union of the soul with divinity. The dissenting Muslims, or *Sufis*, therefore encoded this idea in their poetry, which may have inspired the troubadours to do the same.

Thus one persuasive theory about the meaning of Courtly Love is that the poems written by the troubadours were an encoded form of the Catharist faith made at a time when they were being persecuted. Decoded, this would mean that the Lady who was to be served and loved was nothing less than a form of the Divine Feminine, first recognized as Sophia, and later as Maria, the Virgin Mother of Christ.

Mariolatry

We saw in Chapter 5 how the knight served his Lady in pursuing his ideal of chivalrous duty. In Jungian psychological terms, she personified his *anima*, the feminine aspect of a man's psyche, linked to the soul. By honouring her, and braving perils in order to win her, he was serving – and therefore integrating – this feminine element in himself. However, when the ideal of Courtly Love became entwined with that of chivalry in the Arthurian legends, the sublime aspect of the Lady became confused with that of the Virgin Mary. According to Jung, after that the knight's attempts to relate to the anima were abandoned; instead he began projecting his anima onto the figure of Mary.

The problem with this was that Mary represented perfect goodness. Unlike the Celtic Goddess, she could not embody dual aspects of personality. Her negative aspect therefore became split off, manifesting itself, for example, in the belief in witches.

Today, although the persecution of witches is a thing of the past, the split in the anima still manifests in the extremes of virgin and whore. Many men still see women in terms of these stereotypes. Unless a man can integrate his inner feminine, he will be unable to relate to a real woman, and will be held back in his own inner development.

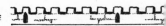

APPLICATION

WOMEN AND AUTONOMY

It is tempting for women to conform to a man's illusions. Every woman is flattered by being the object of worship and tries at some level to provoke it. The reason for this is not just vanity; in the past it has often been the only way she could achieve recognition or respect. But now that women are beginning to become accepted and respected in their own right, it is time for them to let go of the perfect goddess image.

It is also time women stopped expecting men to be perfect heroes. Women who expect to be rescued by a man at any level, emotionally, financially or psychologically, must learn to take responsibility for themselves by developing their inner masculine.

MEN AND INTEGRATION OF THE INNER FEMININE

If you are continually being attracted to unsuitable partners, it is time to look within and assess your relationship with your inner feminine. Until you have integrated the inner feminine, you will go on projecting your anima onto women and then finding fault with them when they prove to be human.

A sign of a well-integrated anima is when a man can express his feelings properly and without sentimentality, is flexible, subtle and imaginative and has an awareness of the natural world. Creative exercises can help you begin this process. For example, you might like to write a poem or short story from a woman's point of view. Try to see the universe through her eyes. What is important to her and why? What do you feel when you begin looking at places, situations or relationships from a feminine perspective?

7

LOVE TRIANGLES

*Passion-pale they met
And greeted: hands in hands, and eye to eye ...
Stammering and staring: it was their last hour,
A madness of farewells.*[17]

LANCELOT

Lancelot is perhaps the first modern hero, a highly attractive figure. His passion for Queen Guinevere is readily understood by those who read romantic novels today. Yet while he easily relates to the present day, his origins go back into ancient time.

Although Lancelot burst into fame as Guinevere's lover in Chrétien de Troyes' story *The Knight of the Cart*, earlier stories of him are quite different. One of the earliest is *Lanzelet*, a translation by Ulrich von Zatzikhoven of a lost Anglo-Norman romance. In this account, Lancelot is the son of King Ban of Benoic, in Brittany, but when his father dies, he is abducted by a water faery and taken to her golden castle on the Island of Maidens. This is an island inhabited by ten thousand women, where it is always spring and no one grows old. In fact it strongly resembles the Celtic Land of Youth.

In this account the 15-year-old Lancelot is armed by his foster-mother and sent to Arthur's court to become a knight. Although in this story he defends Guinevere on one occasion, there is no mention of love or adultery between them. Instead Lancelot enjoys a couple of affairs before settling down and marrying the lovely Iblis.

The version in the *Vulgate Cycle* makes Lancelot's abductor the Lady of the Lake, who takes him to her underwater palace. The story makes it clear, though, that the water is mere illusion. Those at court had experience of mass hypnotism practised by itinerant *tregetours* or conjurors, so this idea would have been understood. A modern interpretation would be that the water is a symbol of the unconscious and that Lancelot was being initiated into the mysteries which lie beneath the surface of things.

Lancelot has also been associated with the Irish God Lugh, who is a solar deity, and with Llwch Llauynnaug, a member of Arthur's warrior band. Also with Llenlleawg the Irishman who helped Arthur capture the Otherworld cauldron in *Preiddeu Annwn* (see Chapter 9).

ChRÉTIEN'S VERSION

Chrétien's story seems to be an amalgam of von Zatzikhoven's account and the abduction of Guinevere by King Malvas in the *Life of St Gildas* (see Chapter 1). By putting the two together he created the love story between Lancelot and the Queen. This was probably suggested by Chrétien's patron Marie de Champagne. In fact, some of the passages describing Lancelot's devotion to the Queen are so extreme that it is possible they were intended as an ironic comment on the Courtly Love ideal.

In Chrétien's version, Guinevere is abducted by Meleagant, son of Bademagu, King of Gorre, or the Glass Island, where she is imprisoned. Both Gawain and an unknown knight (revealed as Lancelot much later in the story) go after her. The unknown knight loses his horse and, after a momentary hesitation, accepts a ride in a cart driven by a dwarf. This is considered a shameful ride because the cart is used for criminals.

After sheltering in a castle for the night and sampling the famous Perilous Bed (which is visited at midnight by a flaming lance), Lancelot and Gawain meet a maiden who demands love in return for information. Gawain readily agrees, but Lancelot prefers to stay faithful to Queen Guinevere.

The maiden tells them of two routes to the island, one by the deeply submerged Water Bridge, the other by the Sword Bridge, which consists of the naked edge of a sword turned upwards. Gawain chooses the former and Lancelot the latter. He arrives on the island, badly lacerated because he has refused to wear armour. The noble King Bademagu offers him a period of rest and ointment for his wounds, but Lancelot opts to take on the king's evil son straight away. The sight of Guinevere watching from a window gives him the strength to win the combat, but he is cut to the heart when she refuses to receive him afterwards. It later transpires that she has heard of his hesitation before getting into the shameful cart.

Lancelot goes off to rescue Gawain, who has fallen off the Water Bridge, while Guinevere suddenly regrets her harshness and attempts to kill herself. Believing she is dead, Lancelot tries to kill himself too, but fortunately he is prevented and ends up forcing the bars apart on Guinevere's window and making love to her passionately for the first time. He escapes detection only because suspicion falls on Sir Kay.

After another battle with Meleagant, Lancelot is betrayed by Meleagant's dwarf and imprisoned so that he cannot fight the return match. There follows a tournament which Lancelot manages to attend incognito but in which he has to obey Guinevere's capricious demands for him to fight badly and then well. After this the story is completed by another writer, who ends it with Lancelot finally killing Meleagant.

Although it seems that Chrétien has mixed feelings about producing this version of the story at the request of Marie de Champagne, nevertheless he obviously relishes the lovemaking between Lancelot and the Queen:

> Now Lancelot has all he desires, when the queen welcomes his company and intimacy, with him holding her in his arms and she embracing him. He finds her lovemaking so sweet and splendid as they kiss and fondle that they truly come to experience such joy and wonderment that its equal was never heard or known.[18]

Chrétien was the first to introduce the story of the adultery of Lancelot and Guinevere. The idea of Guinevere's infidelity was not

entirely new, however. In Geoffrey of Monmouth's version she lives adulterously with Mordred, who has seized the crown prior to the Last Battle. In Chrétien's story the kingdom is not threatened by Guinevere's adultery. Nevertheless Chrétien belittles Arthur by making Lancelot Guinevere's rescuer. The Celts needed a glorious hero figure, but the French Court felt that a powerful love-story was more exciting. Marie de Champagne was primarily concerned with Courtly Love and this version of the story served her purpose.

Adultery in the Vulgate Cycle

As might be imagined, the Cistercian monks took a more serious view of Guinevere's adultery. It is in the *Vulgate Cycle* that she expresses regret that she had ever been born. The guilt attached to adultery affects Lancelot too: he loses his place as the best knight in the kingdom and is hindered in his quest for the Grail. Sympathy for the lovers is eclipsed as the story moves forward into the quest of the Grail and onto a more spiritual footing. The clever idea of the engendering of Galahad introduces an even more perfect knight than Lancelot, but one who is pure and therefore sexless.

The seriousness with which the *Vulgate Cycle* treats Lancelot's affair with Guinevere foreshadows Malory's treatment of the theme in his *Morte D'Arthur*. Here, the condemning of Guinevere to be burnt at the stake and her rescue by Lancelot leads to war between Arthur and Lancelot, which opens the way for Mordred's rebellion and the end of the kingdom.

Nevertheless, Lancelot's devotion to his Queen and his exclusive service to her make him an object of admiration, even in the *Vulgate Cycle*. His struggle between loyalty to his king and passion for Guinevere can be seen as representing the old order – in which a vassal's loyalty to his lord was supreme – giving way to a new order in which women were accorded that devotion. Lancelot's case is complicated by his feeling for Arthur and his personal idealism. His love for Guinevere borders on the spiritual but is finally shown to be misplaced and so prevents him from attaining the Grail.

TRISTAN AND ISEULT

The story of Tristan and Iseult dates from at least 1000 CE. It was not originally connected with Arthur but later became linked to the knightly legends surrounding him. Tristan is not a typical medieval knight. He does not joust or demonstrate chivalric prowess; instead he has great agility and is a skilled harper, which suggests a more Celtic figure.

There were many versions of the story, varying in detail. The main points, however, are as follows. Tristan, nephew of King Mark of Cornwall, goes to Ireland to bring Iseult back to wed Mark, but on the voyage home he and Iseult drink the love-potion intended for her nuptial night and become infatuated with each other.

Iseult marries the King but keeps up a clandestine affair with Tristan. After some time Mark discovers them and condemns them both to death. Miraculously they manage to escape and run off together, living in the woods for three years. After this time Mark wishes to be reconciled with them and Iseult returns to him while Tristan journeys to Brittany. There he meets Iseult of the White

Howard Pyle's depiction of the Royal Bard entitled, 'Sir Tristram harpeth before King Mark'.

Hands and marries her, but on their wedding night a jasper ring given to him by Iseult slips from his finger reminding him of his love for her. He therefore refuses to consummate his marriage.

Tristan is later wounded by a poisoned arrow and, dying, he sends for Queen Iseult to come to him. Although her boat bears a white sail as arranged, his jealous wife tells him it is black. Thinking Iseult is not coming he dies without finally seeing her. When Iseult arrives she dies, grief-stricken, beside him.

This powerful love-in-death theme has reverberated down the centuries. The name, Tristan, means 'sad one'. The theme of noble suffering for love is the same as that of Lancelot and Guinevere. In fact, the two heroes, Tristan and Lancelot, have many features in common. Both are orphaned, both fall in love with the wife of the King they serve and both are torn by conflicting loyalties. But the introduction of the love potion makes Tristan and Iseult more obvious victims of fate. It shows love as a supernatural force visiting unsuspecting humans and sweeping them into a new sphere where the natural laws of loyalty, honesty and constancy no longer apply.

Diarmuid of the Love-spot

The supernatural motif can also be found in the earlier Celtic story of the Irish lovers Diarmuid and Grainne. They, too, are driven by a supernatural power into a fatal love. The young and handsome Diarmuid bears a love-spot on his brow which makes him irresistible to women. He therefore wears a cap to hide it, but one day his cap slips and Grainne, who is betrothed to the elderly King Finn mac Cumhail, comes under the spell of the love-spot.

Powerfully attracted to Diarmuid, Grainne forces him to elope with her by placing him under a *geis* – a magical obligation which cannot be refused. The couple run off and are pursued by Finn. In this story, they escape him and marry, even having children, but when Grainne eventually seeks reconciliation with Finn, she awakens his dormant jealousy so that he lures Diarmuid to the mountain of Ben

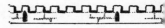

Bulben, where the young man is fatally gored by a magical boar. Although Finn has the power to save Diarmuid by pouring water on him from a nearby well, he refuses to do so until it is too late. After this the story ends prosaically with Grainne eventually deciding to cut her losses and marry Finn after all.

The supernatural

In both these early tales, the supernatural element gives a clue to the origins of the notion of romantic love, the legacy of which has come down to us today. In both cases the pairs of lovers are visited by a force outside their control and swept up into an experience which has its own set of rules. So, when Tristan and Iseult drink the magic potion they enter a new dimension, seeing each other, not just as lovable or sexual objects, but as the completion of themselves, as the fulfilment of a longed-for state of being, and as a means of transcendence. In other words they seek in each other nothing less than spiritual fulfilment.

Lancelot is the first modern hero because he is the first man to suffer romantic love without the intervention of a supernatural agent. Although his story may have been intended as an ironic comment on the mistaken confusion between sexual love and love of the soul, many people have taken his experience seriously. Today the words 'romance' and 'love' have become interchangeable as terms denoting conjugal or erotic love. Yet the Courtly Love ethic held that the sexual act was a violation of 'romantic' love and that the lady who was the object of adoration had to remain carnally out of reach.

Love-in-death

The three heroes Tristan, Diarmuid and Lancelot all experienced sexual union with their unobtainable women and, in so doing, lived a double life, driven by conflict and suffering and even wishing for death. In this context the death-wish is not so strange. It is a form of the desire for transformation. In spiritual terms, death is the gateway to new life. The presence of love-in-death is yet another proof of the spiritual nature of their love experiences. It is also a response to the impossibility of trying to live in another dimension at the same time as trying to conduct a normal life on earth. Because the erotic relationship was overloaded with the spiritual, the love in each case became overwhelming and ultimately fatal.

COUNTING THE COST OF THE ROMANTIC DREAM

Modern readers of these romances find themselves identifying with the lovers and excusing their deceitful behaviour. There is a recognition that they must be excused, as they are living under different and, perhaps, higher laws. They are also not fully in control of the situation, they have been visited by a kind of divine madness which is too powerful to resist.

Yet, looking closely at their relationship it becomes obvious that they do not really seek the good or happiness of the other. Rather they seek in the other a means for self-transportation to the spiritual dimension. This is shown by the fact that if one of them begins to settle down in this world, the other will revive the 'suffering love' at all costs.

A glimpse of this cost is seen when Tristan and Iseult have been parted for some time and she seems to be settling into her marriage, while he allows himself to become betrothed to another Iseult. But on his wedding night, just when a healthier union is within reach, he forcefully catapults himself into his suffering again. In honouring his unattainable love he dishonours and snubs his earthly wife, devaluing the love she offers him. He also betrays and dishonours his king.

Lancelot, too, spurns the women who offer him a viable relationship and instead obsessively serves a woman he can never marry. He, too, becomes traitor to his king. This, in a man of such knightliness and nobility, gives rise to intolerable conflict but, eventually, he is prepared to renounce all other claims except Guinevere's. In *Perlesvaus* when he is told by a hermit that his adultery makes him a traitor to his king and an enemy of God he replies:

> So dearly do I love her that I wish not even that any will should come to me to renounce her love, and God is so sweet and so full of right merciful mildness, as good men bear witness, that He will have pity upon us, for never no treason have I done toward her, nor she toward me.[19]

This assertion demonstrates his total confusion between the erotic and the spiritual.

application

Otherworldly passion

Passionate, erotic love is still the nearest that most people get to a transfiguring experience. But no one can sustain that level of emotion on a daily basis. The everyday task of living with a partner requires a very different understanding of the concept of love, which can still be passionate but without being burdened by unrealistic expectations. Without this understanding, many are tempted to leave their families, lured away by a blaze of Otherworldly passion for another partner who seems to offer them the fulfilment they crave, only to find that this, too, burns out, leaving them dissatisfied.

Perhaps, today, with the tools of psychology to help us, and the free availability of alternative spiritual disciplines, we can begin to disconnect the two kinds of love, human and divine, which have become so unhealthily linked. Perhaps it is also time we stopped admiring Lancelot and Guinevere, and Tristan and Iseult, and began instead to pity them and learn from their stories.

8

THE ROLE OF
WOMEN

… Olwen came, dressed in a flame-red silk robe, with a torque of red gold round her neck, studded with precious pearls and rubies. Her hair was yellower than broom, her skin whiter than sea-foam, her palms and fingers were whiter than shoots of marsh trefoil against the sand of a welling spring. Neither the eye of a mewed hawk nor the eye of a thrice-mewed falcon was fairer than hers; her breasts were whiter than the breast of a white swan, her cheeks were redder than the reddest foxgloves, and anyone who saw her would fall deeply in love. Wherever she went four white trefoils appeared behind her.[20]

This poetic description from the Celtic story *How Culhwch Won Olwen* is taken mostly from Nature. In fact, by the end, it is difficult to tell which is the maiden and which the flower. Elsewhere in the *Mabinogion*, another beautiful woman, Blodeuwedd, is created entirely from 'flowers of oak and broom and meadowsweet'.[21] These women are types of the Nature Goddess or Great Mother who was worshipped by the Celts. She was the supreme Goddess who, each year, took a king or consort who would be challenged at the year's end, killed and replaced by a more vigorous partner (see Chapter 1).

In the story of *Culhwch and Olwen*, Olwen's father, the giant Ysbaddaden, sets impossible tasks for Culhwch to achieve in order to win his daughter. But elsewhere in the story, on arrival at Arthur's court, Culhwch is offered 'a woman to sleep with' along with 'hot peppered chops and an abundance of wine'.[22] This demonstrates

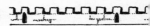

that in Celtic times there was a clear split between the role of the ordinary woman and that of the Goddess who demanded superhuman feats of prowess.

Woman as anima

To modern man, worship of the Goddess is more readily understood on an inner psychological level. As noted in Chapter 6, Jung coined the word *anima* for the inner feminine, or soul of a man. But, like the Celtic Nature goddess, she exhibits both positive and negative qualities.

In the legends it can easily be seen that there are two types of women, each of whom represents these dual aspects of the knight's anima. There is the lady who is imprisoned and needs rescuing, like Dame Lyonesse, but who acts as both his goal and his inspiration and for whose sake he undergoes stringent tests of character and manhood; and there is the faery woman who sometimes uses her powers to help him and other times seeks to imprison him in realms of fantasy.

The negative anima figure often appears in Celtic myth as a beautiful goddess who lures a hero to an Otherworldly island or Land of Youth. In Arthurian legend the hero would be lured away by the erotic qualities of a faery, and would be imprisoned in an enclosed place such as a castle or garden, symbolizing female sexuality.

The positive anima figure in Celtic myth was often connected to a well, spring or river, as the source of life. As we have seen in the story of *Owain and the Countess of the Fountain* (Chapter 4), the Countess is clearly such a figure. She is guardian of the well and appears at the threshold of her kingdom. She marries the hero, who promptly returns to the real world and forgets her, whereupon she punishes him for his neglectful treatment of her.

The woman who was loved too much

In the tale of *Erec and Enide* (also known as *Geraint and Enid*) the hero falls into the opposing trap. Erec becomes so devoted to his wife, Enide, that he loses all interest in taking part in tournaments and demonstrating his prowess. This tale is particularly unusual because Enide is his wife and not an unattainable figure. Also, instead of welcoming his attention, Enide makes him correct his behaviour by alerting him to the criticism of the court.

Reacting violently to Enide's suggestion that he resume his heroic life, Eric immediately sets off to prove himself, taking her with him. He goes to ridiculous lengths to demonstrate his prowess and tries to prevent her warning and advising him. Nevertheless she alerts him every time danger approaches. In the end, rejecting her help and counsel, he overbalances on the side of heroism and encounters Arthur, who considers him to have lost his senses. Finally, after almost dying of wounds, he is reunited with Enide and is happier than before.

Although the tales of *Owain* and *Erec and Enide* seem very different, in both of them the hero experiences a form of madness when unrelated to his Lady. And in both tales the hero is seen to be seeking the correct balance with the inner feminine.

Morgan le Fey, wicked enchantress or healer?

Of all the bewitching anima figures in the Arthurian cycle, Morgan le Fey is the most famous. She is first mentioned in Geoffrey's *Vita Merlini* but there she is the chief of nine holy women on the isle of Avalon and is one of the maidens who tends the dying Arthur after the Battle of Camlann. In Geoffrey's version, she falls in love with

Arthur. Geoffrey does not suggest she is his sister or that she is an evil or scheming figure. She is, however, an enchanter and healer. It is Chrétien who first maintains that she is half-sister to Arthur and it is in the *Vulgate Cycle* that she is turned into an evil sorceress. This was because the Christian author could not entirely condone a female magician or prophet.

So in later legend Morgan becomes a negative figure. She has learned the arts of enchantment and shape-shifting but uses her powers wickedly, excelling as a mistress of temptation and disguises. She is married to Urien and is the mother of Owain. She has a lover called Accolon whom she persuades to make an attempt on the life of Arthur. At one time she falls in love with Lancelot and captures him but he eventually escapes. At the same time, some of her earlier positive qualities remain. For example, when Arthur dies, Morgan is one of the maidens who tends him and takes him to the Otherworld. So she is a complex, dual-natured figure.

Her duality is seen clearly in the story of *Gawain and the Green Knight*, where she is the hidden orchestrator of Gawain's test. She is both the old crone and, it is thought, the Green Knight's wife who tempts Gawain erotically and gives him the kisses and the magic girdle. Apart from secretly keeping the girdle, he acquits himself sufficiently well to save his life so that, at the end of the story, Morgan becomes the more positive challenger of his knightly prowess rather than the evil destroyer.

The complex figure of Morgan le Fey is in some ways linked to another beautiful Otherworldly faerie woman, Nimue.

Nimue

Nimue was also called Viviane and later became identified with The Lady of the Lake, or at least, with one of her damsels. It was she who famously learned her art from Merlin and, at the same time, made him promise not to use any magic against her. He was so infatuated by her beauty that he granted her request. When she had

learned from him all that she needed, she used her powers to imprison him in a chamber from which he could never be rescued.

After that she took over Merlin's role as Arthur's magical protector, particularly against the schemes of Morgan le Fey. For all his prowess Arthur seems to have been ill-equipped to defend himself against the wiles of his half-sister, whereas Nimue is a match for her.

Nimue and Morgan seem to be linked together as light and dark forces. Nimue assists Arthur by giving him Excalibur with its life-preserving scabbard, whereas Morgan steals the scabbard from him and throws it in a lake. Nimue also saves Arthur from Morgan's attempts on his life. When Morgan sends him a poisoned cloak as a gift, Nimue prevents him wearing it. When Morgan gives his sword Excalibur to Sir Accolon, who uses it against him, Nimue magically restores it to him.

Later, Nimue marries Sir Pelleas and lives at court. She saves Guinevere when she is falsely accused of killing Sir Patrise with a poisoned apple, intended for Gawain. Finally, together with Morgan, she is one of the four queens who bears the dying Arthur away to Avalon.

The story of Nimue can be seen as the transfer of magical power from male to female. Merlin gave his power away, showing he was no match for feminine wiles. Arthur, too, had no idea how to combat Morgan's deadly schemes. So perhaps it was appropriate that a female enchanter should take over his guardianship at that time.

Morgause

Morgause was the sister of Morgan le Fey, and another half-sister of Arthur's. Early in his reign, before realizing who she was, he slept with her and she conceived Mordred. Merlin told him that he had sown the seeds of the destruction of the kingdom. Although she does not actively scheme against him like Morgan, she seals his fate by giving birth to Mordred.

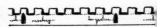

Arthur seems to be shadowed by negative feminine figures, especially those closely related to him. It is only when he is borne away, dying, that he is finally able to receive nurture from them.

BRISEN

Dame Brisen was a very powerful enchantress who performed a function parallel to that of Merlin. Whereas Merlin enchanted Uther Pendragon to look like Igraine's husband Gorlois, and so contrived the birth of Arthur; Brisen enchanted the Grail Maiden, Elaine, to look like Guinevere so that Lancelot would sleep with her and engender Galahad. These were radical supernatural interferences, and demonstrate the belief that Otherworldly agencies had power over natural laws to determine fate.

Brisen contrives this enchantment a second time with the result that Lancelot, realizing he has been tricked again, loses his senses and wanders mad in the forest. Brisen seems to take responsibility for this and magically causes him to be healed, through the agency of the Grail. Since Brisen is linked to Elaine, the Grail Maiden, and to Elaine's father King Pelles, it is not surprising that her powers are connected to the Grail.

The Grail Maiden

Elaine, daughter of King Pelles and bearer of the Grail, is described by Lancelot as one of the fairest women he has ever seen. This is one reason why he forgives her for deceiving him after their night of passion together. He sees her naked the next morning and is unable to be angry with her. He also recognizes that she is wise. Elaine, for her part, acts with the certainty that Galahad is destined to be born and therefore has no fear when Lancelot at first raises his sword to her.

Although she has a great passion for Lancelot, she is aware of her own status and has no thought of allowing herself to die like the

Maid of Astolat (see below). Instead she confronts Guinevere and reprimands her for not being content with King Arthur and for preventing Lancelot from loving a more available woman, such as herself. She points out, reasonably, that now that he has gone mad, they have both lost him. She then leaves Brisen to rescue and heal him.

Elaine demonstrates strength of intellect. Symbolically she represents regeneration, both as Grail Maiden and as mother of the most perfect knight, Galahad. Her wisdom combines well with the intuitive powers of Brisen. Together they form a balanced team for the guardianship of the Grail.

The Maid of Astolat

Another Elaine, known as Elaine le Blank, daughter of Sir Bernard of Astolat, behaves very differently on encountering Lancelot. He is entering a joust incognito and she persuades him to wear her red sleeve on his helmet. He only agrees because he thinks it will help his disguise. When he is badly wounded and taken to a hermit's cell to recover, Elaine discovers his identity and his whereabouts and attends him day and night until he recovers. She then begs him to marry her, or at least become her lover. He courteously refuses her. Eventually she wastes away for love of him and is found by Arthur's court floating dead in a barge, bearing a letter for Lancelot in her hand.

This image of the tragic heroine has been immortalized in Tennyson's poem, *The Lady of Shalott* and also in Pre-Raphaelite painting. Tennyson famously depicted her as being unable to see reality, only images in her mirror. This presupposes that she was a victim of illusion.

The Maid of Astolat is perhaps the most pathetic woman in the stories of Arthur. She gives herself over entirely to Lancelot and, when he refuses her, she has nothing left to live for. The other women – wives, lovers and, especially, enchantresses – while appearing to be passive, are often found to be quietly orchestrating events. A key story in the Arthurian Tradition reveals their ultimate desire.

Sir Gawain and the Loathly Lady

The story of *The Loathly Lady or The Lady Ragnell* tells how Arthur is tricked by his half-sister, Morgan le Fey, into encountering the fearsome knight Gromer Somer Joure, who overthrows him and spares his life only on the understanding that he will return in a year and a day with the answer to the question, 'What is it that women most desire in this world?'

Arthur spends a year collecting possible answers such as: clothes, love, luxury and idleness, but then encounters a wizened old hag who says she knows the right answer but will give it to him only on the condition that he grants her whatever she asks. This he gladly agrees to do. When he encounters Gromer Somer Joure he tells him that what women desire most of all is to rule over men. This is the correct answer so his life is saved, but now he is obliged to grant the Loathly Lady's request.

She asks for the hand of one of his knights in marriage, and all shrink back in horror except Gawain, who honourably offers to take her on. The wedding is a miserable affair. Afterwards when they retire to their bedchamber he can hardly bear to look at her. She asks him for a kiss and he forces himself to oblige her, whereupon she is suddenly transformed into a beautiful woman.

She explains that she has been under an enchantment but that she is now half released from it. For half the day she will be fair, and the other half, foul. She asks him to choose whether to have her foul by day so that the other knights will mock and pity him, and fair by night so that he may enjoy her, or the other way around. He leaves the choice to her and in so doing breaks the spell completely.

This story ends with the outworking of the answer to the riddle. Gawain is the supreme example of courtliness in that he gives the final power of choice to the woman he has married. This story was later used by Chaucer as the *Wife of Bath's Tale*.

The story of the Loathly Lady also links with an early Celtic story of Niall of Ireland, who becomes king because he alone is prepared to

kiss a horrible black hag or *cailleach* who guards a well. By his kiss she is transformed into the Sovereign of Ireland, and she bestows on him the Kingship of Tara.

GUINEVERE

The concept of sovereignty is crucial when it comes to Queen Guinevere. She is the most prominent woman in the whole of the Arthurian tradition. She corresponds to the ancient Celtic Goddess, being a type of 'flower bride'. This was made clear in the tale of her being captured by King Melvas, King of the Summer lands, and taken to Glastonbury where she languished for a year before being rescued by Arthur.

On a larger scale the story of Guinevere's love affair with Lancelot demonstrates the same theme. When Arthur tries to have her burnt at the stake and Lancelot rescues her, the same ritual is being enacted. She symbolizes the sovereignty of Britain. When her life is threatened and neither Arthur nor Lancelot is finally able to claim her, the kingdom of Logres (England) is weakened and war breaks out. Then when Mordred captures her before the last battle, she is left to defend herself as best she can in a fortified castle.

Queen Guinevere is therefore a key figure in terms of the health of the kingdom. Before Chrétien de Troyes invented the tale of Lancelot, she was not necessarily considered an adulterous queen. But the tales of her abduction by at least two knights are very ancient. She had several champions among the knights of the Round Table. This was to ensure her safety, for she held the power of fertility of the land. Once her husband and her main champion failed her, the whole realm became affected.

In the ancient Welsh Triads she is referred to as one of three Guineveres, which again shows that she is linked with the Celtic triple-aspected mother goddess. Her name *Gwenhwyfar* means 'White Spirit' and some sources suggest she may also be associated with the Celtic *Epona* or horse goddess.

APPLICATION

VISUALIZATION OF GWENHWYFAR, TRIPLE GODDESS, WHITE SPIRIT

You are sitting on the bank of a lake. In the middle of the lake is a small island. It is early evening and already the outlines of the island are becoming misty. Through the mist you think you see the form of a beautiful woman. She is standing on the island with her arms outstretched, her long dress flowing over the bracken. Her skin is oyster-pale like the petals of a flower.

As you watch, the light thickens and now she appears as a tree, her outstretched arms becoming brown and gnarled, her neck sinewy. Now again, as you watch, she slowly metamorphoses into stone. She seems serene, timeless, maternal, all-encompassing like some heavy granite sculpture. You feel reassured. And then she begins to turn into petals again, youthful, bewitching, beautiful.

Wait for her face to become clear and then ask her what she wishes to tell you. She may answer by summoning an image or planting a word in your mind. Watch as she turns again into the old woman. Now you may receive more guidance. Watch again and be comforted by her mother aspect. She may have another word or image for you, or even a strong feeling.

As you watch her slowly changing from one aspect into another, become aware of the impermanence of all things. Also remember that what may seem cruel or dark can have a positive aspect to it. For this reason, do not be too hasty in your judgements or reactions but wait for events to turn out as they will. This meditation is to help you to develop an inner detachment. You are seeking the inner wisdom of the Goddess.

And now, as you watch, the darkness gathers and she slowly fades, until all that remains is a wraith of white mist. Take a deep breath and open your eyes.

9 ТHE GRAIL QUESТ

The Grail Quest took the knights of the Round Table into an area
so shrouded in mystery that it still intrigues us today. The first
account by Chrétien de Troyes was unfinished at his death. This has
allowed various endings and interpretations to be added to the
original tale. Such is the nature of the Grail legend that it seems to
be able to bear all the numerous explanations, symbolism and
esoteric bodies of knowledge attached to it.

The first question that immediately arises is what was the Grail
originally? Was it a cup, a plate, a stone or a Celtic cauldron? Also
what was it doing in the court of King Arthur? And finally what
meaning might it still have for us today?

CeLТIC ORIGINS

The cauldron of the Dagda was one of the four mystical symbols
revered by the Celts (see Chapter 4). It had two magical properties.
It could produce unlimited supplies of food and it could regenerate
life. It is associated with the cauldron given to the King of Ireland by
Bran the ancient king or god of Britain whose head was buried at
the Tower of London in order to guard the land. Another magic
cauldron in Celtic mythology is that of the enchantress Ceridwen,
which bestowed the gifts of prophecy and inspiration on the great
Welsh bard Taliesin.

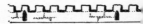

Taliesin himself is the author of the early poem *Preiddeu Annwn* in which Arthur and his companions set off in the ship *Prydwen* to recover a mysterious pearl-rimmed cauldron guarded by nine Celtic priestesses in the Otherworld kingdom of *Annwn*. Its properties included perpetual nourishment and fertility. They make seven expeditions and at the end only seven warriors return. It is not known if they ever found the cauldron, but it may be the same cauldron that Bran tries to bring back from Ireland in the *Mabinogion*. Other Celtic sources speak of the magical cup of the sea-god Manannan mac Lir, which had discriminatory properties in that it would break into pieces if a lie were told over it.

From Celtic sources, then, we have the idea of a magic cauldron, a severed head and a discriminatory cup. All these motifs reappear in the various retellings of the Grail story.

The earliest stories

Chrétien's story, *Perceval*, is generally considered to be the first account of the Grail Quest, but there is a similar story, *Peredur*, in the *Mabinogion*. As with the other stories, it is not known which came first or whether they were written independently using a third source, now lost.

Chrétien's story tells how Perceval was brought up in a forest in Wales near Snowdon by his mother, who deliberately kept him ignorant of the world outside the forest because his brothers had been knights and had all been killed. One day Perceval encounters a posse of knights in the forest and in his naivety he mistakes them for angels. Learning who they are he immediately decides to become one himself. As he sets off for Arthur's court his mother falls into a dead faint, but he rides away without attending to her.

At Arthur's court he is judged unready for knighthood and is sent away to prove himself. After several adventures in which his naivety is embarassingly displayed but he is shown to be a strong fighter, he is taken on by Gornemant, a knight who teaches him the rules of

chivalry and how to fight in proper armour. He then knights him but cautions him in general not to ask too many questions, as it is better and more knightly to display reticence.

At this point in the story Perceval finally begins to wonder about his mother and intends to visit her. But he is delayed by encountering Blancheflor, with whom he falls in love. Finally he sets out for home but on trying to cross a river he accepts hospitality from a fisherman who takes him to his castle. There he discovers the fisherman is lord of the castle but is also crippled.

This 'Fisher King' gives Perceval a sword, after which the Grail Procession enters the room. It consists of a young man carrying a white lance that drips blood, a maiden carrying a radiant Grail made of gold and precious stones, and another maiden carrying a silver carving dish. Perceval keeps silent on seeing it, remembering Gornemant's caution.

After this experience he attends Arthur's Court and is given a hero's welcome. Then an ugly hag comes into the hall and upbraids Perceval for failing to ask the vital question concerning the meaning of the Grail Procession. Because he has failed in this, the Fisher King will not be healed, the land will be laid waste and all manner of destruction will come about.

Perceval immediately undertakes a quest to encounter the Grail a second time in order to ask the correct questions. Five years later he is still on the same quest, but a hermit has told him his failure is connected with his treatment of his mother who died, heartbroken, when he rode away. At this point the story moves to Gawain's Grail quest but eventually breaks off, unfinished.

Although the story of Peredur in the *Mabinogion* is similar, the Grail Procession is more primitive and bloody. It consists of a huge spear shedding three streams of blood and a man's severed head on a dish. It was also greeted with a loud din of lamentation whereas Chrétien's Grail Procession is much more positive and refined.

Symbolic elements in the story

The earliest symbolic elements of the story are esoteric and intriguing. Beside the procession itself, the Quest journeys typically feature a forest, a Waste Land, a chapel, a Grail Castle, a maimed Fisher King and an unasked ritual question. The Grail itself is always carried by a maiden. This, taken with the Celtic symbolic significance of the cup, suggests it is a feminine symbol and, as such, represents what is mysterious, nurturing and unconscious. Certainly the Grail is a source of mystical nourishment, but it is also discriminatory.

The Grail Christianized

In Robert de Boron's version and in the *Vulgate Cycle*, the Grail becomes the cup that Christ passed around at the Last Supper and also the cup which Joseph of Arimathea used to collect Christ's blood when he was pierced by a lance on the cross. The legend of Joseph of Arimathea bringing this cup to Glastonbury became a strong part of the Grail tradition and also gave rise to the winter-flowering Holy Thorn and the Chalice Well, which can still be visited.

Individual quests

The Grail canon describes several individual quests in detail. The main questors are Perceval, Gawain, Lancelot, Bors and Galahad. There is also a little-known story of Perceval's sister setting out on the quest but yielding her life on the way. The other figures have varying success. Lancelot is allowed a vision of the Grail but he may not come too near because of his adultery with Guinevere. Gawain

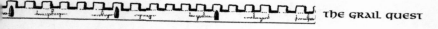

is also turned away, perhaps because he is too worldly. These two fail in their quest but fail impressively.

Sir Bors is perhaps the most down-to-earth character who achieves the Quest and lives to tell the tale. He is a stalwart man who refuses to be seduced by a clutch of maidens in a castle and, after this and many adventures, he finally wins through.

Perceval succeeds to a great extent, partly because of his initial naivety, although this does at times hinder him too. He seems to have a childlike innocence which helps him. But it was famously he who failed to ask the question concerning the meaning of the Grail that would have healed the Fisher King and, by extension, the Waste Land.

Lancelot and his son, Galahad, born of the Grail maiden, were said to be related to Joseph of Arimathea, so it is not surprising that Galahad is the one who achieves the proper vision of the Grail. It is so complete, however, that he dies on seeing it, overcome by ecstasy.

Links with the East

In some accounts of the quest the three successful knights are taken in a magical ship, the Ship of Solomon. This is not surprising when one considers the strong connections with the East which came about because of the Crusades. There was even mention of an original source of the Grail legend coming from the East. Such hints are given by Wolfram von Eschenbach, a German poet who wrote *Parzival*, perhaps the most symbolic and esoteric account of the Grail legend. He sees the Grail as a green stone which fell from heaven. He says its secret was known to a Jewish astronomer called Flegetanis who was versed in alchemy and the mysteries of the East and who discovered the story of the Grail in ancient Arabic lore.

GUARDIANS OF THE GRAIL

The Templars were knights who had taken part in the First Crusade. In 1118 they formed an order for the protection of pilgrims to the Holy Land. Originally there were only nine of them and they followed the monkish rule of poverty, chastity and obedience. The order expanded and they became the bankers for the Crusaders.

After Jerusalem was taken by Saladin in 1187, the role of the Templars should have ceased, but by then they had thousands of properties and had been accorded religious immunities by the Pope. They had become a secret society whose members swore allegiance to each other rather than to king or country. Eventually their wealth and autonomy attracted opposition. Charges were made against them of secret and devilish rites. In 1307 Philip IV of France imprisoned six hundred of them and secured enough confessions under torture to justify his public burning of Jacques de Molay, the Grand Master, and Geoffrey de Charney, the Preceptor of Normandy.

Various reasons are given for this extreme attempt to wipe out the Templars. It is true that to some extent their order had become corrupted by wealth, but there were more powerful reasons. Their wealth, which Philip attempted to seize was, of course, a strong factor, but it is also thought that they had become guardians and promoters of a secret religion which they may have received from the Manicheans and Gnostics of the Near East.

Like the Cathars, the Templars were considered a threat by the Catholic Church. Word was that they were also the guardians of the original treasure found at the site of Solomon's Temple. They received warnings just before Philip made his sweeping arrests and much of their treasure was spirited away by sea. Some of it is thought to have been brought to Scotland where the Templars had allies in the powerful Scottish family, the St Clairs.

One of the most fascinating buildings associated with the Templars is Rosslyn Chapel near Edinburgh, owned by the St Clairs and considered by some to be the Grail Chapel. Interest centres on the very fine 'Apprentice Pillar', which stands out amongst the wealth of symbolic carving. Some believe the original Grail chalice came over to Scotland with the Temple treasures and is now hidden either in a sealed vault beneath the chapel or inside the Apprentice Pillar itself.

The former Languedoc area of France, which was associated with the Cathars and Mary Magdalene, is another possible hiding place for the original Grail. Certainly the mystery remains to be solved. The Templars' secrets are thought to have been passed on to such orders as the Rosicrucians and the Freemasons. It seems the Templars were guardians of both the actual Grail and its symbolic meaning, an inner *gnosis*.

The Grail and Arthur

In some respects the story of the Holy Grail sits uneasily within the Arthurian canon. It is the ultimate quest for the knights and, for many, a hopeless one. The flower of Arthur's knights go after it and the fellowship of the Round Table is effectively broken.

Yet, in other respects, the Arthurian setting is the only one capable of bearing such a story. We have seen how the individual quests of the knights made them autonomous figures in their search for self-mastery. Their only religious consellors were the holy hermits they met at remote shrines on their journeys – remnants of the ancient Celtic monastic settlements. This alternative source of religious teaching provided an appropriate setting for the mysterious Grail – which symbolized the culmination of the individual religious quest. Also, the idea of the Grail was especially attractive at a time when the communion cup was withheld from the laity by an edict issued by Innocent III in 1215. The Grail chalice, by contrast, was available to all.

The Grail and the Catholic Church

The popularity of the tales would have been a source of worry for the Church were it not for the fact that they attracted candidates for the Crusades. The result was that the stories were accepted by the Church, Arthur was made a champion of Christ and the Grail was Christianized as Christ's cup. However, despite this, some of the old pagan beliefs associated with the Grail remain within the stories.

Application

Grail quest

In the faint moonlight, the grass is singing
Over the tumbled graves, about the chapel
There is the empty chapel, only the wind's home

T. S. Eliot's poem *The Waste Land* was inspired by the legend of the Holy Grail. In the last verse he says, 'I sat upon the shore/ Fishing, with the arid plain behind me.' These powerful images, the chapel, the Waste Land, the Fisher King and the Grail itself, are all potent today. The land is still waste – today literally as well as spiritually.

The question concerning the meaning of the Grail has still not been properly asked, so the search for the Grail continues. Whether it can be discovered in its material form is debatable but it is still a powerful symbol for all those who feel drawn to the life of the spirit. Many people today are still setting out on the Grail quest, recognizing that the way may sometimes be lonely and hard, but also that there are surprises and new discoveries waiting to be made.

The Grail quest is a personal and individual one. It is a quest for self-discovery and self-mastery, the attainment of wisdom and inner healing. It is a journey towards the transcendence of the soul. It represents love, both human and divine, and honours individual human striving for higher understanding. Each person will experience the Grail in the form appropriate to his or her inner being. Yet everyone who undertakes it comes to understand a common symbolic language and to appreciate a common history.

If you wish to embark on this quest yourself, you may find it helpful to read about the different quests made by Arthur's knights. (You can find more detailed information about these in the companion book in this series, *The Holy Grail – A Beginner's Guide.*) Each of their quests reflect their different characters and it may be that you identify with one more than another. You might start with a visualization in which you imagine yourself setting out and your chosen knight accompanying you. The Grail is a symbol large enough to accommodate many and various spiritual ideologies. As such it can be seen as offering inspiration to all.

10

THE RETURN
OF ARTHUR

*In her own chamber she placed the King on a golden bed, with
her own noble hand she uncovered the wound and gazed at it
long. At last she said, health would return to him if he were to
stay with her for a long time.*[23]

Malory's great triumph was to make the story of Arthur's death
overtop that of Lancelot and Guinevere. The story is poignant,
mysterious, open-ended. Malory begins by telling how the night
before the Battle of Camlann the dead Sir Gawain comes to Arthur
in a dream and warns him not to fight because the slaughter will be
horrific and he will be killed. Next morning Arthur consults his wise
men and they decide to try to make a treaty with Mordred. Both
armies send fourteen knights into the field to negotiate, but there is
so much suspicion of treachery that when one of the knights, bitten
by an adder, draws his sword, this single act sets off the fighting.

A full-scale battle ensues in which nearly all the knights on both
sides are killed. At the end Arthur sees Mordred leaning on his
sword among the dead bodies. He runs at him and thrusts his spear
into him but, with a superhuman effort, Mordred heaves himself up
the shaft of Arthur's spear and thrusts his sword through Arthur's
helmet into his brain.

Fainting and on the point of death, with nearly all his knights slain,
Arthur is left with only Bedivere to help him. The dying king
commands Bedivere to take his sword Excalibur and throw it into
the lake. Twice Bedivere tries to do this, but the workmanship on the
sword is so exquisite that he hides it instead. The third time Arthur
sends him, however, he hurls the sword across the lake, and it is

92

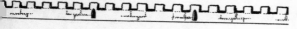

caught by a woman's hand and brandished three times before
disappearing under the water. This powerful and magical image of
Kingship Returned is given full treatment by Tennyson in his *Morte
D'Arthur*:

> The great brand
> *Made lightnings in the splendour of the moon,*
> *And flashing round and round, and whirl'd in an arch,*
> *Shot like a streamer of the northern morn,*
> *Seen where the moving isles of winter shock*
> *By night, with noises of the northern sea.*
> *So flash'd and fell the brand Excalibur:*
> *But ere he dipt the surface, rose an arm*
> *Clothed in white samite, mystic, wonderful,*
> *And caught him by the hilt, and brandish'd him*
> *Three times, and drew him under in the mere.*

Then Arthur asks to be taken quickly to the lakeside, where a dark
barge filled with black-hooded maidens has appeared on the water
and is moving towards him. The women weep and shriek when they
see him. Bedivere puts him into the barge and one of the women,
Morgan le Fey, lays his head in her lap saying: 'Ah, dear brother,
why have ye tarried so long from me?' The barge then disappears
from sight.

AvaLon

Malory says Arthur was taken in the barge to Avalon. Geoffrey of
Monmouth in his *History* says: 'Arthur himself, our renowned King,
was mortally wounded and was carried off to the Isle of Avalon, so
that his wounds might be attended to.'[24] In the *Vita Merlini* he
describes Avalon as an Island of Apples, a fairy island, dwelling
place of nine mystical women, presided over by Morgan le Fey.

The fairy island recalls all those Celtic Otherworldly islands and
Lands of Youth. The number nine was a mystical number for the
Celts, but in Geoffrey of Monmouth's account, it could also refer to
a community of nine female druids once said to live on the Isle de

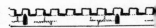

Sein, off the coast of Brittany. They possessed magical and healing powers and received the souls of the dead.

Arthur's return

Nearly all the main accounts say that Arthur will return. Malory states that he can find no certainty of Arthur's death and that many people believe he shall come again. Both Wace and Geoffrey of Monmouth say that Arthur was carried away to Avalon but that he will come again. Layamon ends his account: 'But whilom was a sage hight Merlin; he said … that an Arthur should yet come to help the English.'[25] And William of Malmesbury concluded 'the tomb of Arthur is nowhere to be seen, wherefore the ancient songs fable that he is yet to come.'[26]

The seven sleepers

A tale is told that once in the hills of Gwynedd, a shepherd boy stumbled upon a cave entrance under a hazel tree and, crawling into the cave, came upon a circle of seven knights sleeping and Arthur himself sitting asleep at a stone table in the middle of them. His hair and fingernails had grown long, and a horn and sword lay beside him on the table. When the boy tried to lift the sword Arthur, half-roused from sleep, demanded to know if it was yet time, whereupon the boy ran away in fear. Afterwards he tried to find the cave entrance again, but never succeeded.

Other versions of the story have the boy blowing the horn twice and half-waking the sleepers who again demand, 'Is it time?' But the boy flees rather than daring to blow the horn a third time and wake them completely.

The idea of an enchanted cave in which Arthur lies with his best knights, ready to wake and defend the land in need, is a powerful one and brings us back full circle to the Celtic origins of his kingship. The Celtic belief that the king was wedded to the Goddess and, through her, to the land, accords well with the fact that Arthur considered himself protector of Britain. It is even said that he ordered the digging up of the head of Bran (the ancient Celtic god whose head was buried near the Tower of London) on the grounds that he, Arthur, was the new protector of the land. So it is perhaps fitting that he should himself be lying in a cave waiting to defend Britain in her hour of need.

Arthur in art and Literature

Meanwhile this 'once and future king' has been perpetually renewed in art and literature. His stories provided the inspiration for Spenser's *The Faerie Queene* in which he portrayed Elizabeth I as Gloriana, who presides over twelve knights symbolizing twelve different virtues, who each undertake a different adventure. In the seventeenth century Milton considered writing an epic on Arthur, but decided instead to write *Paradise Lost*.

Then, after suffering a decline, the Arthurian Tradition was resurrected in the nineteenth century as part of the Romantic Movement. In the wake of the Industrial Revolution the age of Arthur appeared to poets, composers and artists as an idyllic, golden and heroic era. The Pre-Raphaelites looked back to that age to give them inspiration for a portrayal of beauty to combat the ugliness of industrial Britain. Their paintings depict idealized knights and beautiful ladies in perfect rural landscapes. Wagner was inspired to write his opera *Parsifal* and, perhaps most famous of all, Tennyson was inspired to write *Idylls of the King*.

Tennyson studied Malory, the *Mabinogion* and Layamon, among others, before writing *Idylls*. Such was its popularity that 10,000 copies were sold in six weeks. His magnificent *Morte d'Arthur* was included in the poems but was later published separately as well. After that he wrote many more poems on the Arthurian Tradition with varying success. His *Morte d'Arthur*, however, is still one of the most moving accounts of the closing of a golden era. At the end of it

we stand alone, like Bedivere, in a kind of bleak darkness while the King and all he symbolized slowly recede into the distance:

> Long stood Sir Bedivere
> Revolving many memories, till the hull
> Looked one black dot against the verge of dawn,
> And on the mere the wailing died away.

In contemporary writing Arthur has become a Celtic hero again. He has been depicted with extraordinary force by David Jones both in his paintings and in his two books *In Parenthesis* and *The Anathemata*. His poems are an emotional and esoteric amalgam of ancient Celtic and Arthurian themes. Other twentieth-century poets who have addressed this theme include John Masefield and Charles Williams.

However, Arthur is more often the subject of contemporary novels. In many of these the wistfulness following Arthur's death, so poignantly evoked in Tennyson's *Morte d'Arthur*, is still evident. At the end of Bernard Cornwell's *Excalibur*, the Saxon, Derfel, has become Arthur's companion and watches the dying king disappear with the same sense of loneliness and isolation as Tennyson's Bedivere. T. H. White ends his classic set of four novels famously entitled *The Once and Future King* with his own quiet hope that Arthur and his knights will return when not only England but the whole world needs them.

The women novelists show a similar wistfulness. Rosemary Sutcliffe has given a famous and beautifully human portrayal of Arthur in *The Sword at Sunset*, in which the passing of his idealized kingdom is still something to mourn. Marion Zimmer Bradley ends *The Mists of Avalon*, her first-person account of Morgaine (Morgan le Fey), with her brother's head in her lap, heavy with approaching death. In her understanding, all who die return to the Great Goddess, and are regenerated like the seasons. In Mary Stewart's *The Last Enchantment*, the ending is more allusive but still has a 'dwindling barge', albeit metaphorical, a chair recently vacated by Arthur and, most poignantly, a harp, symbol of the Celtic vision, unstrung.

How Sir Bedivere cast the sword Excalibur into the Lake.

application

Inspiration and creativity

The figure of Arthur has inspired numerous creative artists: painters, writers, composers and poets. He is always surprising and new, yet always recognizable as the ancient model of kingship that we all hold in our imagination.

Write a poem, song or short descriptive passage on the return of Arthur or on aspects of the Otherworld where he might be dwelling. Consider what you would like Arthur to accomplish and what you think the land needs.

CONCLUSION

Every age has turned to Arthur and cloaked him with its chosen mythology. The French needed a chivalric hero and body of courtly knights at a time when it was cultivating a new attitude to women and religion. Henry II needed a mythology to empower the monarchy. Elizabeth I needed to ally herself with a figure representing the might of Britain. The Victorians needed to reinforce their ideals of Christian and family morality and Tennyson shaped his *Idylls of the King* to encompass this. He also suggested that Arthur represents an ideal to strive for, an inspirational standard of excellence. His Arthur represented the human soul fighting against evil.

Not surprisingly, Arthur speaks again to our present age. He speaks in symbols which illuminate our psychological understanding. His knights' quests are relevant within the landscape of the psyche. The rescuing of damsels in castles can be reinterpreted by contemporary

man as a challenge to rescue and recognize the feminine within. The dragons, giants, witches and serpents are the negative forces of greed, ambition, selfishness and lust which must be combated within the self.

He also fosters the spiritual life. He was not too proud to listen to Merlin and take his advice on matters that were outside his understanding. He acknowledged the wisdom of the Druidic Magician who had access to deeper truths and realized he had to work with him. Most importantly he recognized the importance of the Grail and encouraged his knights to go after it even at the cost of the Round Table Fellowship. In other words, he yielded up the glory of his earthly kingdom for the possibility of something higher. It is this that marks him out as truly great and why he became, in legend, a type of Christ. It is also why he is still inspirational today.

A very important feature of the modern revival of interest in Arthur is that he is no longer coated in medieval romantic trappings. The comparatively recent discovery of Celtic archaeological sites has brought the Celts nearer to us today. Arthur has been reinstated in his contemporary setting and speaks to us with a new and forceful realism. His link with the land through ritual marriage with the Flower Maiden is again acknowledged. It is good that he champions the land at a time when it is threatened by global forces. If he is two-parts awake in a cave deep within an English or Welsh hillside, maybe now is the time to rouse him fully – or maybe he always returns in his own way when needed, now as ever before.

NOTES

For more details, see Bibliography

[1] Doel, Fran and Geoff, and Lloyd, Terry, *Worlds of Arthur*, pp. 73–4
[2] Matthews, John, *An Arthurian Reader*, p. 270
[3] Jenkins, Elizabeth, *The Mystery of King Arthur*, p. 64
[4] ibid. p. 66
[5] Williams, Gwyn, A., *Excalibur*, p. 53
[6] Tolstoy, Nicolai, *The Quest for Merlin*, p. 28
[7] ibid. p. 75
[8] Malory, *Morte d'Arthur*, Vol.1, p.16
[9] ibid. p. 83
[10] ibid. pp.115–16
[11] Chrétien de Troyes, *Arthurian Romances*, p. 223
[12] Ebutt, M. L., *Ancient Britain*, p. 372
[13] Malory, *Morte d'Arthur*, Vol 1., p. 251
[14] Chrétien de Troyes, *Arthurian Romances*, p. 104
[15] Ovid., The Amores, p. 101
[16] Lindsay, Jack, *The Troubadours and their World*, p. 101
[17] Tennyson, Alfred, *Guinevere*, ll. 98–102
[18] Chrétien de Troyes, *Arthurian Romances*, p. 247
[19] Cavendish, Richard, *King Arthur and the Grail*, p. 87
[20] Gantz, J. *The Mabinogion*, p. 151
[21] ibid., p. 111
[22] ibid., pp. 137–8
[23] Jenkins, Elizabeth, *The Mystery of King Arthur*, p. 62
[24] Geoffrey of Monmouth, *The History of the Kings of Britain*, p. 261
[25] Jenkins, Elizabeth, *The Mystery of King Arthur*, p. 69
[26] Barber, Chris, and Pykitt, David, *Journey to Avalon*, p. 161

SELECT BIBLIOGRAPHY AND DISCOGRAPHY

Barber, Chris, and Pykitt, David, *Journey to Avalon*, Blorenge Books, 1993

Cavendish, Richard, *King Arthur and The Grail*, Book Club Assoc., 1978

De Rougemont, Denis, Princeton University Press, 1983

Doel, Fran and Geoff, and Lloyd, Terry, *Worlds of Arthur*, Tempus, 1998

Ebutt, M. L., *Ancient Britain*, Chancellor Press, 1995

Eliot, T. S., *Selected Poems*, Faber, 1999

Fife, Graeme, *Arthur The King*, BBC Books, 1990

Gantz, Jeffrey (trans.), *The Mabinogion*, Penguin, 1976

Geoffrey of Monmouth, *The History of the Kings of Britain*, Penguin, 1966

Hopkins, Andrea, *Chronicles of King Arthur*, Collins & Brown, 1993

Jenkins, Elizabeth, *The Mystery of King Arthur*, Michael Joseph,1975

Johnson, Robert, A., *The Psychology of Romantic Love*, Arkana, 1983

Lewis, C. S., *The Allegory of Love*, Oxford University Press, 1958

Lindsay, Jack, *The Troubadours and their World*, Frederick Muller, 1976

Loomis, R. S., *The Grail From Celtic Myth to Christian Symbolism*, Columbia University Press, 1963

Malory, Thomas, *Le Morte D'Arthur*, vols. 1 & 2, Penguin, 1969

Matthews, John, *The Arthurian Tradition*, Element, 1995

Matthews, John (ed.), *An Arthurian Reader*, Aquarian Press, 1988

Matthews, John, and Stewart, Bob, *Warriors of Arthur*, Blandford, 1987

Miller, Helen Hill, *The Realms of Arthur*, Peter Davies, 1970

Ovid, *The Erotic Poems*, Penguin, 1982

Tolstoy, Nikolai, *The Quest for Merlin*, Hamish Hamilton, 1996

de Troyes, Chrétien, *Arthurian Romances*, Everyman, 1997

Williams, Gwyn, A., *Excalibur*, BBC Books, 1994

Music

Noirin Ni Riain, *Celtic Soul*, Earth Music Productions, LMUS 0031

Loreena McKennitt, *Parallel Dreams*, Quinlan Road Ltd., Canada, QRCD 103

Celtic Woman (compilation), Celtic Woman Records, CWRCD 7001

Alan Stivell, *Renaissance of the Celtic Harp*, Rounder Records, Mass., CD 3067

Available from C. Hamilton, c/o the publisher, or at: **claire@hamiltonharps.freeserve.co.uk**

Company of Strangers, *Blodeuwedd – A Wife Out of Flowers*, COS 298

Company of Strangers, *The Love-Song of Diarmuid and Grainne*, CSSM1 (cassette)

The Celtic Harp, Claire Hamilton, Sound and Media Ltd, SUMCD 4133

The Celtic Harp Collection, Claire Hamilton, e2 ETD CD/003

Celtic Myths, Claire Hamilton (harp and spoken word), Music Collection International, ETD CD/157

INdEX